The
CANADIAN
GARDENER

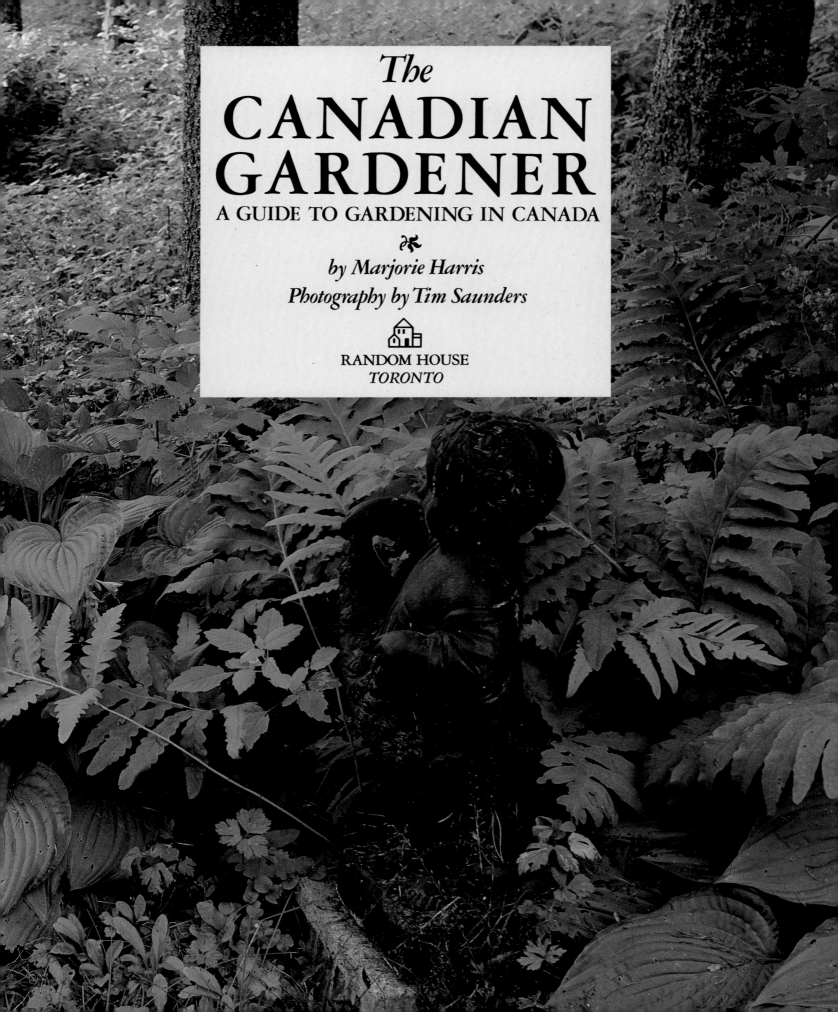

The
CANADIAN
GARDENER

A GUIDE TO GARDENING IN CANADA

by Marjorie Harris

Photography by Tim Saunders

RANDOM HOUSE
TORONTO

Published in Canada in 1990 by Random House of Canada
Limited, Toronto

Canadian Cataloguing in Publication Data

Harris, Marjorie
        The Canadian gardener

ISBN 0-394-22085-4

1. Gardening - Canada. I. Title.

SB453.3.C2H37 1990   635.9'0971   C90-093690-8

The author has tried to be as accurate as possible with information
supplied by gardeners and acknowledged authorities.
We regret any errors or omissions.

Design and art direction: Andrew Smith
Editorial: Barbara Schon
Production co-ordination: Dorothy Franklin
Page make-up/Production: Andrew Smith Graphics Inc.
Line illustrations: Paul Zwolak
Map art: David Chapman
Jacket color separation and film: Colour Technologies
Color separation, printing and binding: New Interlitho S.p.A.

Printed and bound in Italy

Cover:
*(Zone 9) Pierre Archambault and Brent Webber created this graceful
garden of utmost simplicity. Left to right:* ROSA CARDINAL DE RICHELIEU,
TRADESCANTIA VIRGINICA *and a wonderful peony of unknown origin.*

Previous page:
(Zone 6) Arthur Dauphinee has allowed HOSTA FORTUNEI *to spread
naturally through this mysterious woodland garden.*

Foreword, page 7:
*(Zone 8) Margaret Charlton's garden is perched on the side of a steep hill.
This is only one of the ponds on the property.
From left to right:* PAPAVER NUDICAULE, *Iceland Poppy;* PRIMULA JAPONICA;
Deer Fern; ACER PALMATUM ATROPURPUREUM, *Japanese Maple. Not in bloom:*
IRIS; POLYGONUM; TROLLIUS. *In the background:* EUONYMUS COLORATA.

CONTENTS

THE GARDEN SPIRIT
9

GARDEN VARIATIONS
60

SPECIAL GARDENS — SUGGESTIONS AND SOLUTIONS
100

HARDINESS ZONES — SELECTED PLANT LISTINGS
128

ACKNOWLEDGMENTS

To Jack, for the love

To Charlotte, Heather and Juliet
for the cheerleading

Thanks to the Garden Gurus for giving me the benefit of their wisdom and years of experience so generously: Murray Haig who did such a fantastic job of reading the manuscript and making valuable suggestions; and Juliet Mannock who gave me constant encouragement. And thanks to Amanda McConnell, Bob Brown, Neil Turnbull, Sybil McCulloch, Susan Ryley, Walter Ostrom, Captain Dick Steele, Pamela Frost, Penny Arthurs, Kathie Leishman, George Radford, Al Smith, Ernie Lithgoe, David Tomlinson, Marjorie Hancock, Patrick Seymour, Dugald Cameron, Isobelle Downey, Anna Leggatt. All of whom shared good ideas.

For invaluable help in contacts and research: Ann Kemp, Tom Duguay, Ruth Dynbort, Helene Major, Juliet Farrow, Richard Lindseth, Clarence Johnson, F. Leishman, Jeanne Marler, Janet Rosenberg, Sheila Paulson, Jon Lowry, John Wellwood, Sarah Batten, horticultural societies in British Columbia, Alberta and Nova Scotia. And to Chris Harris who provides the brawn in the garden and makes it fun.

The gardeners who let us see and photograph their gardens: Carol Dancer, Jill Robinson, Tom Baskett, John K. Weagle, Stewart McInnes, Donald McInnes, Mr. and Mrs. Gordon Campbell, Enid Webber, Diana Hilchie, Sally Norwood, Mr. and Mrs. Wilfred Stevens, Mr. and Mrs. Neil Harnish, Arthur Dauphinee, Kay Hulme, Walter Ostrom, Sheila Paulson, Roy Lindseth, David Matthews, Phyllis and Fred Enns, Lewis G. Thomas, Ernie Belsek, Sheila Grande, Margon Thiessen, Nadine Crawford, Doris and David Groebel, David Harrup, Ann and Alexander Cross, Mr. and Mrs. Harley Hotchkiss, Dave Matthews, Helga Schmidt, Don Heinbecker, Mr. and Mrs. Cornelson, Murray Haig, Ricky and Victor Shields, John Manuel, Amy and Clare Stewart, Aileen Harris, Midge Ellis Keeble, Lisa Dalholt, Caesar Blake, Dr. Henry Landis, Q.C., Deirdre and David Tomlinson, Shari Creed, Mr. and Mrs. Myron Gottlieb, Amanda and Lawrence Finn, Joanne Shaw, Pat and Rick Howard, Janice and Hugh Rennie, Michael Shulman, Al and Maureen Ross, Ellen Eisenberg, Lynn and Bill Aimers, Deborah Campbell, Barbara Frum, Jeanne Marler, Romulus and Sandra St. Laurent, Lambert De Wit, Betty Piper, Bridget Hutchison, Joan Courtois, Mr. and Mrs. Vladimir Kurgansky, Isabel Gales, Mrs. E. Price, Kathie Leishman, Francisca Darts, Don Armstrong, Thelma Chapman, Mary Stewart, Joan Patterson, Peggy Tupper, Barbara Durrant, Pamela Frost, Jack Todd, Elizabeth England, Margaret Charlton, Pierre Archambault, Shirley Beach, Brent Webber, Al and Shirley Smith, George Armstrong, George Radford, Ernie Lithgoe, George Nation, Joan Patterson, Dr. and Mrs. Felix Lion, Sybil McCulloch, Audrey and Geoff Williams.

The Public Gardens: Van Dusen Gardens, Vancouver; Edmonton's Devonian Botanical Gardens; University of British Columbia Botanical Gardens; Saxe Point Park, Victoria, B.C. Departments of Agriculture who supplied information on climate and soil: *Landscaping Alberta Yard; Shelterbelt Planting and Farmstead Beautification;* Alberta Department of Agriculture; Publications from Agriculture Canada, Ottawa: Dr. Bernard S. Jackson, *Rock Gardening in Newfoundland; Growing Herbaceous Perennials in Newfoundland; Newfoundland Gardening in Peat and Woodland soils,* Oxen Pond Botanic Park, Memorial University of Newfoundland; plus other publications from the Ontario Ministry of Agriculture and Food, and Ontario Agricultural College, University of Guelph. *Saskatchewan Gardening Guide,* Saskatchewan Agriculture. *Herbaceous Perennials for New Brunswick Gardens;* Agriculture Canada, Fredericton Research Station Arboretum; *The Climate for Agriculture in New Brunswick;* New Brunswick Department of Agriculture. *The Climate for Agriculture in Atlantic Canada;* Atlantic Agriculture. *Native Trees and Woodland Shrubs of Prince Edward Island; Soils of Prince Edward Island,* Prince Edward Island Department of Agriculture and Forestry. Publications from Ministry of Agriculture and Fisheries, Province of British Columbia. Publications from the Department of Agriculture, Province of Manitoba.

Map of Plant Hardiness Zones in Canada, compiled by Land Resource Research Institute and Ottawa Research Station, Agriculture Canada.

This book is the result of a team of extraordinary people all of whom are gardeners who understood the obsession of it all: Linda McKnight who put us in touch with Ed Carson, Publisher-extraordinaire; Andrew Smith who designed it and Barbara Schon who edited the manuscript. Never has any group made work more pleasurable.

Marjorie Harris

FOREWORD

Photographer Tim Saunders and I travelled from coast to coast looking at gardens for this book. We were astonished at the variety and excellence of what we saw, and by the generosity of gardeners everywhere. Not only did they let us into their gardens, we usually returned home laden with new plants.

Every shot in this book is extremely personal, reflecting Tim's and my taste. We chose each one for very special reasons. But we had to photograph far too much given the huge distances we were travelling and the fact that there was only one crack at each location. There are many gardens we shot in that aren't represented in this book. That's not because they weren't beautiful—in the final cut—editorial needs and limitations of space dictated what got in. To those gardeners we apologize. To the rest a grateful thank you.

Most people don't read a gardening book from cover to cover. I hope you'll change that habit with this one. I've spread the information around so you won't get overwhelmed by any one topic. Gardening is a lot of fun and I hope that this book will enhance your pleasure and make it easier for you to have a splendid garden.

Marjorie Harris

THE
GARDEN SPIRIT

*I*t was a painting that drew me into gardening. For years it hung on our living room wall, a painting by the Canadian artist Louis de Niverville filled with plants in lush, sensual colors. I loved it, and after some time, figured that, just maybe, I could make a garden that would be like the painting. It was a matter of looking carefully. Or so I thought.

When I began twenty years ago, I had an intellectual vision based solely on art books. From these books and visits to museums, I knew about Persian gardens, Italian Renaissance parterres and Impressionist visions. I learned the long and hard way. Fantasies were replaced by reality. Those books had nothing to do with the piles of weeds that existed in our backyard or the dried-out helpless grass trying to grow in the front. Mine was a typical urban space —more bowling alley than greensward. Not something Monet would have lusted after. I found out that you can muck about in the backyard in a kind of helter-skelter way. Or you can *garden*.

Learning to garden meant learning to trust my own taste. I might never attain the exact picture my imagination has of the garden, but to me it's satisfying and very beautiful as it is. What I've really been doing over these years has been renovating the garden. It's changed as I have and as my needs have evolved.

THE GARDEN GURU

Everyone needs a garden guru—someone you can phone for the wisdom that comes of experience. I'm lucky. I have lots of them, across the country and close at hand. Some of them are professionals, some plantspersons—those most serious of collectors—and others who are merely as obsessed as I am. I get help from them and soak up their ideas, many of which are reflected here.

A guru can be just about anyone whose judgement you respect. You'll find most gardeners are extremely generous with information if you are really interested. But don't go to them wanting to strut your own stuff—you'll just waste their time. Pay attention. You can learn a great deal just talking to these people or observing them at work.

THE INSPIRED GARDEN ❧ Inspiration for your garden renovation can come from almost anywhere. Never be afraid to steal ideas. Get them from the local botanical garden, a neighbor with a spectacular green thumb, from books, from garden tours.

My inspiration came from what I'd call a minor epiphany. We gardeners like to think in large concepts. I was gazing at the back snowscape when I began to visualize paving stones set in a checkerboard pattern. Ah ha, this would capitalize on the long narrow aspect of the garden. It would finally have some sort of definition.

(Zone 5) Through the garden gate of Amy and Clare Stewart one can see SIDALCEA;
and CAMPANULA PERSICIFOLIA, *Bellflower;*
greenery, HYDRANGEA PETIOLARIS, *and right by the gate, hostas.*

What a sensational, original idea, I thought. Highly invasive plants and herbs could be set in the squares, deep borders would contain perennials and shrubs. This design, attractive from every window in the house, would give the place some style. Since then I've seen something similar in books on garden history. Did I remember it unconsciously? I don't know but it doesn't really matter. It works in what was just another ordinary rectangle—a space that has since become animated with amazing possibilities.

I'm suggesting that you start looking at what you've got with new eyes. Don't necessarily settle for something conventional—a few borders marching uniformly along the edges of your garden. You have something special to give gardening and your project is to find out what it is.

First you must eliminate all fear of gardening. People who visit my garden inevitably say, "It must be a lot of work." Yes and no. It depends on your definition of work. I consider this my exercise, my time to myself, a place for meditation. It's pleasure. If work is the number of hours spent slogging away, then it *is* work, but not the kind I resent.

Mostly I think of my garden in terms of what it's given me. Briefly, gardening can instruct you in the ways of nature and how we are inextricably bound together. It makes you sensitive to the smells, colors and sounds of even the most restricted spaces. If you aren't terrified by aesthetics, the garden can train your eye to color and composition better than an art book—and in a shorter time. A garden teaches you about harmony. It might even enhance the value of your property, but since this is all about personal taste that's unpredictable.

And finally you have to lose the fear of the plants themselves. Perennials are tough creatures, prepared to be abused. The will to survive is built into the genetic code of each plant. You'll have to be brutal to destroy that.

To start with, you must decide what you want your garden to do for you. You have to take into account kids, animals, entertaining and time. Especially time. Be singularly honest. How many hours a week or a day do you really want to put into this space? If it's only a few, then work out a plan that has plenty of shrubs, trees and foliage plants, such as grasses, hostas, and ground covers that will require minimal care. Pick on perennials that won't mind a bit of drought.

Have a vision of what you want as I did with my winter epiphany. It took me about three months to work everything out. Months? Well, there is nothing instant about gardening, and never get conned into believing there is. If you want instant, take up squash. If you want a beautiful garden, you need not only time but also method.

I spent many years in my garden without any system at all. I ordered new plants as soon as the January plant catalogues arrived and was first in line when the nurseries finally opened their doors in spring. I'd buy one of everything. But something was always lacking, some sort of grace note.

What the checkerboard gave me was the underpinnings of a design. And that meant I had to put something on paper. Since it was a winter epiphany it didn't interfere with actually being out there working. I don't know why I was so reluctant to do this before. Perhaps I felt it would make gardening too serious, too much of a commitment for my casual nature.

You can draw a garden, you can write a garden and you can describe your garden fantasies to friends. Just make sure you have some idea of what you want before you begin. I started by writing all my thoughts in a memo to myself simply because that's easiest for me. Then I transcribed them roughly into map form on the back of a poster, made a list of all the plants I already had and figured out where they should go in the new scheme. Then I got help with the backbreaking labor of digging the whole place up—essentially a new beginning.

HOW TO START A GARDEN

Absolutely all my best ideas have come from what I call Creative Staring. If you stare long enough you'll visualize what the garden will look like in three years when the plants have matured. You'll see its potential.

While you are leaning on your hoe, or sitting on the deck with a cup of tea or glass of wine, eyes glazed over, staring, you are doing important work. Your mind is sketching out new plans, moving plants from one position to another, or experimenting with a whole new color scheme in an old border.

Next to staring, books are your most important resource, but not just big glossy impossible-to-attain fantasies of the rich and famous. I'm talking about art books. They are jammed with gardens recorded over the ages. You'll be able to pick up useful combinations that might send you off in new directions. What you're looking for is not exact duplication but a mood or a feeling that will help you define your own style.

I'd always fancied paintings of Mediterranean gardens with fruit-laden citrus trees and exquisite year-round foliage and flowers. But what had drawn me to those gardens was the shape—long, narrow, enclosed courtyards; herb gardens bound together by clipped boxwood. A combination of something very tidy and very casual. My kind of garden.

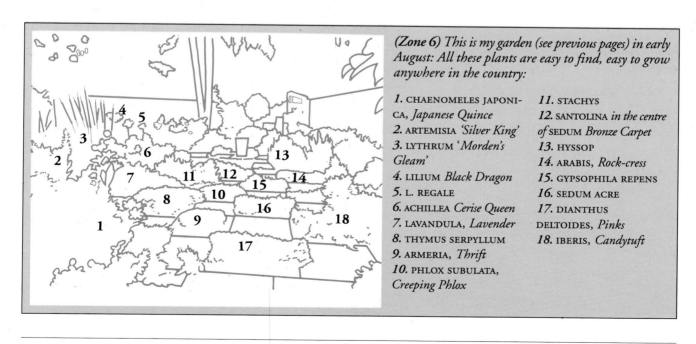

(Zone 6) This is my garden (see previous pages) in early August: All these plants are easy to find, easy to grow anywhere in the country:

1. CHAENOMELES JAPONICA, *Japanese Quince*
2. ARTEMISIA *'Silver King'*
3. LYTHRUM *'Morden's Gleam'*
4. LILIUM *Black Dragon*
5. L. REGALE
6. ACHILLEA *Cerise Queen*
7. LAVANDULA, *Lavender*
8. THYMUS SERPYLLUM
9. ARMERIA, *Thrift*
10. PHLOX SUBULATA, *Creeping Phlox*
11. STACHYS
12. SANTOLINA *in the centre of* SEDUM *Bronze Carpet*
13. HYSSOP
14. ARABIS, *Rock-cress*
15. GYPSOPHILA REPENS
16. SEDUM ACRE
17. DIANTHUS DELTOIDES, *Pinks*
18. IBERIS, *Candytuft*

Then there are the other more obvious places to raid: any public, botanical, or really good private garden nearby is fair game. Talk to these gardeners. They've experimented with the plant material that will grow in your neighborhood. If it does well for them, it's going to do well for you too. It will probably save time and money if you start with planting what they've had growing for years.

The more you look the more acute your eye will become. And ever more critical. You will learn all about divine dissatisfaction when it comes to your own garden. You will also learn to appreciate gardens that aren't your taste but are good in and of themselves.

Take bits and pieces from everywhere. Look carefully at the photographs in this book. We searched for gardens with ideas to help you: pleasing color combinations, graceful ways of putting plants together; gardens that worked on an abstract scale of good design and the possibilities of a soaring imagination hampered only by climate and soil.

Of course following a formula devised by someone else who has never seen your particular garden is almost impossible. You'll find lots of useful books in libraries with designs, plant lists, and recipes for putting things together. But you'll probably never find one that's exactly you. And that's good. Because your garden will look like no one else's since what you bring to it is unique.

PRINCIPLES OF GARDENING

Gardening does not have to be hidebound by rules. But there are a few general principles that will save you grief down the road. They are not carved in stone but come from a sensible approach. I like writer Geoffrey Charlesworth's definition of an experienced gardener as someone "with acquired commonsense."

THE GARDEN AS EXPERIMENT ❧ If you keep in mind that all gardening is a form of experimentation you won't get discouraged. Stuff dies, things come up the wrong way, combinations don't work.

Start modestly. Versailles is not what you're after. The modest approach may irritate you when you are not as successful as your neighbor—gardening does make one a tad competitive—who can grow anything without trying. Or so it seems. Attempt something and if it doesn't work, abandon it. I move flowers in full bloom if the colors aren't right. This is very hard on plants but since I'm giving them such good care in the first place, they usually survive with a little bit of extra nursing. If you take this route be sure to cut the flowers off and water and feed them well.

THINK SHORT AND LONG TERM ❧ Short term is what you want the garden to look like this year and probably for the next two years. Long term is the basis of all your design plans—the trees and shrubs that will outlast your tenure

(Zone 9) Susan Ryley's plant combinations give her garden the pictorial quality you see here.
Top left to right: CYTISUS BATTANDIERI, *Pineapple Broom, Delphinium;* IRIS SIBIRICA;
THALICTRUM AQUILEGIFOLIUM; ERMERUS HIMALAICUS; *Foxtail Lily;*
Bottom left to right: Variegated grass; GERANIUM *Johnson's Blue;* NEPETA MUSSINNII, *Catmint;*
ARTEMISIA ABSINTHIUM, *'Lambrook silver'.*

here. Count on one thing though, you will change your mind constantly as you become experienced and develop your eye. Perfect. A garden evolves.

If you only want a set piece, rather than an evolutionary experiment that develops as you do, you can hire someone else to accomplish the whole. In fact a pro who can stroll through and advise you might prove to be useful. But if you do hire a professional get someone who is prepared to study your garden in detail. A gardener lives in a garden. And it's this living in the garden that provides both the most important information and the enchantment. And never hire anyone who wants to start you off with three foundation plantings and shrubs by each side of the door. No imagination at work there and not worth your while at all.

DESIGN ELEMENTS OF GARDENING

STYLE ❧ The style of your garden can be something formal with carefully clipped grass and elegant borders; an English cottage garden with a jumble of flowers and vegetables; or one centered on water such as a swimming pool, pond or fountain. You may want to concentrate on a single color or combination of colors or perhaps one filled with exotic grasses.

You can also choose the kind of gardener you want to be. A plantsperson collects plants for the love of collecting. It is the pursuit of the unusual and rare plant that makes the game thrilling. Or there is the design-conscious gardener. The person who chooses plants only because they fit into an overall design ignoring all others. And then there is the person who tries to combine both urges: collecting certain kinds of plants but placing them in a pleasing

design. Unless you become obsessed with a certain species, you'll probably end up in the latter camp as you become more sophisticated.

To start the design of my own garden, I eliminated one of my pet hates—grass. It's a boring ground cover. And I don't like the chemicals people pour over it to keep it green and weed-free—all that muck may get into the water table and poison our precious drinking water. I was only too relieved to pull it all up and start again. The shaken-out clumps of grass turned face down created a berm in one part of the garden. Dead flat changed by this slight undulation and—*voilà!*—I've now got some contour. It made a secret place and created new demands.

Feel free to dig down, make ponds, hills and valleys, if you fancy. Add bricks and paving stones to the middle of the garden rather than huddled against the house. In gardening you never have to do the same old thing in the same old way. Be audacious. But keep in mind that you will want to create vistas where you look through one aspect of the garden to another. And make surprises. A turn in the path, a small rockery hidden from view but not from the sun, an arbor to sit in. Just be sure that everything is in scale with the size of the space you have. Scale is crucial to good design.

POTENTIAL ❧ Look at the architecture of your house and the style you've used in your interior design. This is always a good place to start especially if you aren't quite sure what it is you want. A first sensible step would be to reflect these qualities and harmonize them with what you want to do in the garden. Harmony is the key here: a Cape Cod style house with a formal Italian parterre is not harmonious. Take all the

(Zone 6) J. Schofield Manuel's garden.
Cotoneaster falling over the concrete wall; RHODODENDRON CATAWBIENSENSIS ALBUM
and HOSTA ALBOMARGINATA.

good things a site has to offer and get rid of the irritating things if you can.

I'm stuck with a neighbor's gigantic weeping willow that not only blocks the sun but also fills my garden with junk. But when I think of the microclimate this tree creates, the cooling system it provides, and of how it keeps the swampy soil beneath it just at the right moisture level, I'm grateful. Look around you. Capitalize on what your neighbors have got and incorporate their trees and shrubs into your garden. Or barricade yourself from some eyesore with judicious plantings of plump shrubs, weeping trees, solid conifers and vines running rampant.

(Zone 6) Arthur Dauphinee's vista is in complete contrast to the Ryley garden.
The vision through the honeysuckle-covered arbor surrounded by the blue and pink of VERONICA,
Speedwell and LYTHRUM *add to the romantic spirit of the garden.*
To the left: Blue and pink HYDRANGEA MACROPHYLLA.

Opposite: (Zone 9) Susan Ryley has created stunning contrasts in this sensual vista to a fine border in the
rear. Center to the view is a COTINUS COGGYGRIA PURPUREUS, *Smoke Tree;*
ACER PALMATUM 'DISSECTUM', *Japanese maple, cascades beautifully into the water;*
IRIS PALLIDA VARIEGATA *and* I. LAEVIGATA.

*Above: (**Zone 7**) Another special version of a classic garden plant from Francisca Darts' garden* ACHILLEA ABRONTANOIDES, *Yarrow.*

*(**Zone 5**) Isabel Gales' traditional border with willow trees and large drifts makes a sweeping statement in this setting.*
Left to right: Shasta daisies; ACHILLEA *'Moonbeam';* HEMEROCALLIS; LILIUM REGALE; *Delphiniums. In the background are:* ECHINOPS RITRO, *Globe Thistle;* OENOTHERA; FILIPENDULA; MONARDA DIDYMA.
Off to the right: ERYNGIUM, *Sea Holly.*

PRINCIPLES CARVED IN STONE

THE GARDEN AS TEACHER ❧ One immutable law of gardening is that your garden will instruct you. That will come from living in it. You can't impose more things than it can absorb and end up with a graceful result. You cannot, for instance, put in every plant in every catalogue and nursery at your disposal and produce something satisfying. I know this from painful experience. You need a subtext—a color scheme, a family of plants, special foliage. These will eventually begin to define your true style.

GARDENING BY SECTIONS ❧ I can't emphasize enough how important this second immutable law is. Divide your garden into areas that can be worked easily. If you tackle everything at once, you run the risk of being overwhelmed by how much has to be done before you accomplish anything. Take one section of your design and do a smashing job on it. This will encourage you, and let you know if your design is workable. This gives you the latitude to solve problems before you go to the expense of completing the whole design. Gardening by experiment fits right in with this idea.

Don't turn down anything that will logically carve up the space. For example, set up a barrier of lattice work—very ordinary stuff you get at

(Zone 6) Amanda and Laurence Finn's garden, designed by Neil Turnbull. An existing ancient pear tree is espaliered along this handsome fence. The little plants in front are CAMPANULA *'Blue Clips' and* SEDUM *'Autumn Joy'.*

a building supplier's—and cover it with vines. Try a fast-growing one like the annual Scarlet Runner Beans. Then add slower growing vines such as clematis alongside. Choose plants in a variety of colors so that you'll have a succession of bloom right into fall. Plan for all seasons. Perhaps take a shrub such as Japanese Quince, CHAENOMELES JAPONICA, and espalier it—that is, take a plant, choose one strong central branch to go up and a lateral one sideways then cut out everything else. Train them along wires in whatever design you find works well.

You could try a raised bed with big architectural plants such as ERYNGIUM, Sea Holly, or ECHINOPS, Globe Thistle (they are both like elegant thistles and gorgeous); and some of the big-leaf plants such as RHEUM PALMATUM, Ornamental Rhubarb; perhaps some RICINUS COMMUNIS, Castor Beans. Create a bed or an area for some grand and exotic specimens.

Construct a low wall with slabs of rock as a barrier that has to be walked around. A small stand of shrubs will do the same trick. Or a couple of weeping shrubs. In fact any kind of plant barrier will do. Then concentrate on the space in front of this. Leave the rest of the garden until you can tackle it next year.

Begin working with one bed, or border as it's called. If you're extra ambitious perhaps two. Add to them section by section harmonizing one into the other as you proceed. You will be absorbing new ideas in the process. Good design evolves. Keep in mind this is an experiment and nothing more.

LE JARDIN DE REFUSE ❧ The third immutable law is never to be afraid to do something over again. If the plants look wrong rip them out and start over again. Move them around. Being afraid of plants is a waste of time. I have a *jardin de refuse* for those plants that haven't worked out the way I want them to. I reserved a small area 7 x 10 feet (2 x 3 meters) for the wrong reds, the excess of yellow, the extra Shasta Daisies, seed I couldn't identify. Someday they may be incorporated into a new border or given away. I've learned from this you don't have to get overwrought about every single color you put in the garden. This unplanned space looks quite wonderful. And it serves as a great cutting garden.

PLANNING THE GARDEN

Don't be put off by the idea that you have to make a plan. I wish I'd succumbed earlier. You start with the skeleton, the drawing, as it were, for your painting—the existing shrubs and trees in your garden and those of your neighbors' that you will have to work with. Good design is so subtle you barely notice its presence, unlike the way you do style—the cottage or all-blue garden for instance.

Think of an axis to base your placement of these important and expensive plants on, an X or a triangle or a long view that is slightly off center.

This may sound odd but consider winter first. That's when your underpinnings are most noticeable. You want to make them balanced. Put evergreens, vines and shrubs with bright colored stems in vistas you can see everywhere from the house. Make an arrangement that's pleasing whether or not there's any snow. Use plants that will catch and hold snow—a lilac standard for instance—a lilac that's been grafted on to the single stem of a tree will do the trick.

*(**Zone 9**) Here is an enchanting little corner of Shirley Beach's garden.*
Korean Boxwood surrounds a carpet of THYMUS SERPYLLUM.
Top left to right: Rose, Sarah Van Fleet (1926); Rose, Zephirine
Drouhin (Bourbon 1868); LEVERKUSEN, *Climbing Rose (1954);*
white CAMPANULA PERSICIFOLIA; *Hybrid Musk Rose,*
Moonlight (1913).

*To the right: (**Zone 6**) Caesar Blake's garden designed by Murray Haig*
shows the use of repetitive design from higher to lower levels.
This is a good winter garden and is harmonious with its surroundings.
The pattern of the brick echoes the SYRINGA VELUTINA, *lilac standards,*
and EUONYMUS FORTUNEI, *Emerald Gaiety, and* E. SARCOXIE *on the left.*
Dwarf Alberta spruce in the circle with a sculptured WOODWARDIA.
Globe Cedar grows on a lower level underneath the lilacs.

(Zone 6) This garden designed by Janet Rosenberg features from top left:
THUJA OCCIDENTALIS FASTIGIATA, *Pyramidal Cedars;* CALLUNA VULGARIS, *Heather;* ACER DISSECTUM
'ARTROPURPUREUM', *Japanese Red Maple;* PICEA PUNGENS 'GLAUCA GLABOSA', *Globe Blue Spruce;*
CALLUNA VULGARIS, *Heather;* BUXUS, *Boxwood;* PICEA PUNGENS 'GLAUCA', *Colorado Blue Spruce.*

The shrubs and big plants basic to your design will anchor borders or create new areas of interest. Break up a long border with a flowering shrub, or make a corner stand out with an arresting combination of shrubs. Keep things very simple. The old Bauhaus dictum that "less is more" actually works sometimes when it is applied to gardening.

Then comes the mix of plants. And this is the hard part. Look first at the structure of a plant, its architecture if you will. Tall, angular, spreading, or floppy? Get a feel for what you want to put together. Don't just plunk things into holes thoughtlessly. Then the color combinations: subtle harmonies or rich contrasts? What is it that says something to you?

You might want to think like the great English garden designer, Gertrude Jekyll (rhymes with treacle):

Colour, in gardening as in painting, does not mean a garish or startling effect...it means the arrangement of colour with the deliberate intention of producing pictorial effect, whether by means of harmony or contrast.

Take your pick or try both—in different parts of the garden. For instance, you might want to have cool colors near the house and hot colors further away to add greater depth to the garden.

In planning your color schemes, keep in mind that things are going to change every two to three weeks depending on what's in bloom. Perpetual change is one of the basics of gardening. From coast to coast we heard "If only you could have seen it two weeks ago," or "Come back in two weeks." Gardeners are never satisfied. But it's not so much dissatisfaction as divine discontent.

This is all part of the fun. And one of the reasons gardeners tend to be obsessive. They are following a dream, a vision, a fantasy which can be terribly useful. If you're bored at a party all you have to do is transport yourself into your garden. Insomnia? Nothing like slowly drifting through the garden to relax. And you will never be lonely. Plants are great companions.

(Zone 5) Amy Stewart's eye for detail is seen here with ROSA *'New Dawn'; backed by* HEMEROCALLIS, *Daylily; in the urn are* VERBENA *and* HELICHRYSUM PETIOLATUM.

Color and texture inevitably go together. Combine feathery and leathery, grey foliage with different greens. Make a pattern with your colors so that the eye moves gently across the landscape. I've been in some gardens that make me jittery. "These are all very nice plants," you muse, "so why is my eye darting about?" Usually it's because too many elements are at work. Strong colors may be dotted all over the place without any *raison d'être*. Or the contrasts may be horrific. Or blotchy plantings—areas of plants here and there without any logic. Eventually it'll give you a headache.

THE MIX ❧ Learn to mix your plants. If you have nothing but perennials you will have a short-lived garden since they bloom for about three to five weeks. You may want a fantastic climax and not care about anything after that but it's a bit like sex, most of us like to prolong the best for as long as possible. To bring color to the garden throughout the season try biennials that have foliage this year and bloom next year, and annuals that have one glorious season and then die.

Choose your perennials with an eye to the different blooming periods from earliest spring to fall. Then use the annuals and biennials to fill in the gaps.

HOW TO CHOOSE A PLANT ❧ One concept is to take a family of plants and learn about it. Build your garden plant by plant. I have never been able to do this. I have too often lusted after the last thing I read about. Restraint seems to come with experience.

And like everyone else, I have prejudices. There are colors I actively dislike and plants I don't seem to get along with. I am not a rosarian though I do admire roses in other people's gardens. I can understand being obsessed with roses. But they are not for me.

However, I can understand getting hooked on collecting a specific genera. SEMPERVIVUM, Hen-and-chickens, otherwise known as Houseleeks, would be perfect for someone who has a container or balcony garden. There are dozens of different kinds; they are subtle, beautiful; don't take up much space; and they won't succumb to high-rise winds.

Over the years my initial yearning for a hot garden has cooled down considerably. Thus many of the strong reds and yellows have been moved to the *jardin de refuse*. For instance, I find I love anything with grey foliage because it provides light and softness. All grey plants adore the sun so I have space for them. I'm fascinated by ARTEMISIAS and I'd like every CAMPANULA I can get my hands on.

The more I garden, the more I tend to love the species of a plant family. These are the original plants, the parents of all the hybrids. They tend to come in simpler, purer shapes. If you compare a species rhododendron with one of the great overwhelming hybrids you'll see what I mean. There is something rather tender and intimate about a species plant.

Blue is my favorite color so I tend to have accents of blue. But I wouldn't necessarily want an all-blue garden or even an all-white garden. I still like pinks and magentas somewhere out there. But as I keep emphasizing, the garden evolves in an unending experiment.

Choose a color you particularly like and find out about the plants in that range. You'll discover that no two pinks or whites are alike. Put them together and add something as a foil: a plant with feathery foliage or one of my favorites, the greys.

Select plants because you want to attract birds and bees to your garden. You can think up any number of themes to be part of the sub-text. But always, always think about the foliage. Every garden is in foliage most of the time. But you'll be amazed at the subtlety once you get to appreciate the infinite variations of green. And try grey in sunny areas as a lovely foil. (See The Foliage Garden, page 78.)

The most significant factor in your choice of plants is the necessity to combine those with similar requirements. Put desert plants with desert plants, for instance, and try to imitate their natural environment. Eventually, this will cut down on maintenance. (See The Natural Garden, page 64.)

DESIGNING A BORDER

Any group of plants in a bed is called a border even if it isn't bordering anything. Tradition says a border should be from 6 to 10 feet deep

(2 to 3 meters) and 25 to 200 feet long (7.5 to 60 meters), obviously depending on the size of your garden. Tradition says that tall plants should be at the back, medium in the middle and little ones at the edge. Tradition says that island borders (something in the middle of the garden) should have tall plants at the center and smaller ones around them. But tradition is just that—something always done in the same way because it works rather well. You can experiment with round, kidney-shaped, square or even fluted borders. Make sure, however, that they are in scale with the whole area and don't look fiddly—ragged edges bopping in and out crazily for no reason at all. Borders should have a flow to them and not look like they've been parachuted in from someone else's place.

THE CONTEXT ❧ What really works is something with good proportions. You can work it out on paper, or by eye using hoses or rope to get something pleasing. Just don't make it so big you can't take care of it easily.

In a small garden, an 8 x 20 foot

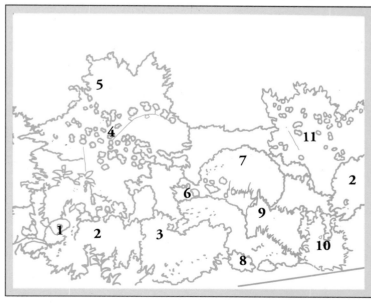

(Zone 9) Color harmonies are beautifully articulated in Susan Ryley's garden (see previous pages). You wouldn't think that the red of the rose standard would work so well with this group, but it is brilliant in this situation:

1. PAPAVER ORIENTALE, *Oriental Poppy*
2. GERANIUM MAGNIFICUM
3. G. *Johnson's Blue*
4. ROSA MOYESII *sp. standard*
5. Black Stem Bamboo
6. Pink Peony double

7. GILLENIA TRIFOLIATA
8. HEUCHERA CYLINDRICA
9. BAPTISIA AUSTRALIS
10. STACHYS LANATA
11. CYTISUS BATTANDIERI, *Pineapple broom*

(3 x 6 meters) border is very manageable and it allows you to get into it without stepping on plants or compacting the soil while trampling around in there to reach inaccessible plants. In a slightly larger garden, a border 45 x 15 feet (13.5 x 4.5 meters) with access from both sides would be dramatic. Proportion is what to keep in mind. A tiny cutout in a huge space will trivialize any design. If you've got an expanse to work with think in grand terms, make a statement with huge borders. If you have a small garden think in intimate almost courtyard concepts and keep it simple.

There is a lot of talk about the necessity for *drifts* of flowers. Three of the great designers of this century, Gertrude Jekyll, Russell Page and Christopher Lloyd, recommend them highly—massing of one kind of plant usually in an elongated shape with more plants in the middle and tapering at each end. That's a statement and a sensational idea if you've got a huge garden. Otherwise content yourself with putting in two or three for effect. If that looks spotty, add some more. And bear in mind the size of the plant in a few years. Things like ACHILLEA, Yarrow, just get bigger and blowzier. I couldn't even take a patch of three in my little garden—it would look overgrown. One is just fine.

But don't make the mistake I did and have one of everything. I finally figured out that's why some of my former gardens made me so dissatisfied. And never think of plants in isolation. Work within the context of the whole. Be aware of what you're putting each plant next to. You want fluidity and movement—the choreography of the garden.

Scale, always critical, is also true with plants. One gigantic plant out of place can upset the balance. Since this isn't a life and death situation, does it even matter? You might like a startling effect. After a while though, as your garden sense develops, you'll find it's rattling to have this oppressive creature dominating the scene. Take pampas grass. An imposing plant indeed. It looks dumb shoved up against a foundation wall or jammed into a tiny garden. The best use I've seen was at the end of a long vista beside some water. Once again we have context.

AN UNBREAKABLE RULE ❧ Never, ever put plants in tacky little rows, or hideous groups of rectangles or squares. Bunch them together, make elongated shapes but don't have them marching about like little soldiers in straight lines. You do not want to end up with a garden that even vaguely resembles municipal planting. You might even want to steer clear of their favorite combinations of red salvia, white petunias and yellow zinnias; or a teeth-gnashing combination of hot purple and brilliant orange. Death.

I tend to jam in too many plants because I want to cover as much bare ground as possible and get an effect as quickly as possible. But I

(Zone 9) Shirley Beach put her garden together rose by rose.
Tucked in one corner is this little bench surrounded by German Bearded Iris: From center top left to right: Bourbon Rose, Adam Messerich (1920); CLEMATIS VITICELLA, *Abundance, climbing up standard* LABURNUM; ARTEMISIA, *Powis Castle on either side of the bench; in the center Damask Rose Leda.*

(Zone 6) Left to right: In Walter Ostrom's garden RHODODENDRON, *'Ramapo'; Dwarf Heather;*
R. XANTHOCODON; R. YAKUSIMANUM; R. KIUSIANUM.

don't crowd plants that will be unhappy if they are moved in a year or two.

Annuals, however, are different—I stuff them in and don't worry about them. Their job is to fill in the empty spaces left by perennials gone out of bloom. Since they only have one year to live, it might as well be glorious. Perhaps use one kind of flower in all its different colors and this will give you some kind of scale. If you should happen to choose petunias—I wouldn't, can't stand them—cut them right back after flowering and they'll bloom again for you. So will most other annuals, but more on that later under deadheading.

When Jekyll rearranged her borders she used to carry a flower around and put it against others to see how it would look: good contrast? a foil? a blend? It's still a pretty good method to help in making decisions.

SOME FAVORITE ANNUALS ✺ These plants are all lovely fillers and some have a tendency to self-seed if you let them—which I do to a limited extent. Love-in-a-mist; larkspur; nasturtium (especially a seductive rose shade); CLEOME; African Daisy; California and Shirley poppies; candytuft; and of course impatiens planted in clumps of five or six to form impressive little bushes by midsummer; wallflower, ornamental tobacco and stock, for scent.

HOW TO GET INTO THE GARDEN

First thing you do before going into the garden is some serious stretching. You wouldn't go on to the tennis court without a warm-up: knee bends, toe touching, and long stretches. Gardening is a lot more taxing than tennis. Make it part of your gardening ritual. While you're in the garden keep on doing these stretches. I haven't seen very many tubby gardeners. And there are mortality tables to prove that dedicated gardeners live longer. So there.

Don't be upset if your spouse or mate loathes gardening. When there's a couple in the garden one automatically becomes the brains, the other the brawn. Be happy that you are stuck with it on your own. However, since this is a capital improvement on the property you can demand at the least the cost of some help. You will certainly need some brawn in the initial preparation and I'm all for getting help when it's needed. Being either a slave or a martyr to the garden detracts from its essential pleasure.

GARDEN EQUIPMENT

All great passions require some kind of equipment and gardening is no exception. Unlike a lot of other hobbies you don't have to break the bank to participate. And there are no annual dues. In fact, it's much wiser to put your money where it shows—in the plants—rather than on stuff that you may or may not use. Buy equipment slowly. It can be expensive. Only buy a tool when you feel it will make your efforts more effective. Then buy the best you can.

WHAT NOT TO BUY ❧ A very, very expensive pair of trousers with pads and pockets making you look like a yokel. Not necessary. Or kneeling pads that strap to your legs. They slide down and the elastics that are supposed to hold them on have to be so tight you'll get varicose veins. Use a rubber pad or piece of styrofoam. Evil-looking machines called weeder-eaters. You roll them over the ground to rout weeds. They may be useful in a vegetable garden but aren't for the flower garden.

(**Zone 9**) *Susan Ryley uses white and yellow with accents of grey to make the colors stand out.* ALCHEMILLA VULGARIS; *Roman Wormwood;* LYSIMACHIA NUMMULARIA, *Creeping Jenny; Golden Mock Orange; Bowles' Golden Grass;* HELICHRYSUM ANGUSTIFOLIUM; ROSA *'My Pet';* PANACETUM; PARTHENIUM *'Aureum', Golden Feverfew.*

(Zone 7) VIBURNUM TOMENTOSUM *'Cascade' from Francisca Darts' garden is a particularly beautiful version of this useful shrub.*

To the left: (Zone 6) J. Schofield Manuel's garden designed by Murray Haig. The garden view is extended by the mirror. Left to right: SORBARIA, SORBIFOLIA, *False spirea,* RHODODENDRON CATAWBIENSE 'ALBA'; HYDRANGEA PETIOLARIS; *Sweet Alyssum;* DRACAENA *and Sweet Alyssum in the pot; hosta; dwarf* WOODWARDII; *Cedars flanking the mirror planted with* ASPERULA ODORATA, *Sweet Woodruff.*

WHAT TO WEAR 🌿 Baggy old pants, a loose shirt and a sun hat. The sun hat is a must. Once you get into the garden, you may lose track of time and become seriously burned on the back of the neck. There are clogs specially designed to wear in the garden that many superb gardeners wear. I haven't invested in them yet—old sandals are fine for the moment

WHAT TO BUY 🌿 Shovels, spades, trowels must be made from a single piece of steel, not welded, and should have the strongest wooden handles possible. If you amortize the cost of a good garden spade over the number of years you'll use it, there's no point in picking up a cheapy at the local hardware. Good equipment is a good investment.

HERE'S WHAT I USE CONSTANTLY

Transplanting trowel: Buy this before you get anything else. It has a long dished blade and is perfect for making holes and getting into difficult spots. You'll also need a heavy-duty trowel for heavy-duty jobs.

Garden spade: Smaller than an ordinary spade, it's lightweight with a sharp straight blade. Good for dividing plants as well as digging them up.

Hand cultivator: This three-pronged instrument is used to scratch the earth around plants and haul out weeds. You can also get one with a long handle and both are useful.

Garden fork: Has sharp slightly angled tines to lift large chunks of soil without putting out your back.

Rake: Both the long floppy type to take up leaves and the one with short hard tines.

Twig broom: These are common in Europe.

They are ancient artifacts that look like witch's brooms. I've never found anything more effective in cleaning up a garden. And almost impossible to find in North America. One substitute: bundle up some cedar boughs and tie them together. It works, but not as efficiently as a good old twig broom.

Secateurs: Clippers, shears whatever you want to call them. Buy a superb pair and take care of them. You can also get a belt holder so they are always with you.

Bonsai scissors: These funny-looking Japanese scissors aren't an absolute necessity. I like using them for fine cutting work on flowers. They make deadheading a pleasure.

Plant identifiers: Plastic or metal sticks to put near your plants. The plastic ones break easily and the metal are expensive. Get something. You'll need them because many plants seem to disappear during winter and you won't know what's what in the spring—friend or foe.

Gardening gloves: Another must. I like goatskin gloves because the lanolin they contain makes your hands feel good, not like prickly pears. They wash up easily and last for years. There are stretchy numbers that cover the hand like a second skin. These are also good. You've got to have some protection because a pierce from the thorn of a rosebush, for instance, can lead to serious infection. I know a woman who almost lost her hand. We are never so near to death as in the garden is one of those horticultural aphorisms that contains the truth.

I tend to carry hand tools around in an old basket. I'd leave anything fancy and beyond this list to other people to give you as gifts. With gardening becoming big business, a thousand temptations will be thrown in your path. Resist most of them. The old ways still work.

THE REAL WORK

Getting your hands dirty is one of the splendid things about gardening. I can spot a fellow gardener at a party by the condition of his or her nails. We gladly give up well-manicured hands from April to October. Use good old Vaseline to keep them relatively civilized.

THE SOIL ☙ By now you will be on intimate terms with your garden. Never mind whether you want to do something simple or elaborate, before you do anything at all check the soil. This is the earth's skin and like all skin wants to protect itself. Thus we have weeds—to hold in moisture, and keep the topsoil intact. The function of the gardener is to get rid of those weeds and make the decision of what plants to replace them with. Try the following in each section:

Take a handful of moist dirt and squeeze it. You can figure out what kind of soil you have by the way it feels.

Sandy—loose, falls apart immediately.

Clay—thick, heavy, comes out in hard chunks or makes a slick path when you streak it.

Silt—doesn't crumble.

Loam—holds its shape.

If you don't have loam you'll need to improve your soil. (See Ecological Garden, page 48.)

Have your soil tested for acidity or alkalinity. This is called the pH (potential hydrogen or hydrogen ion concentration) and you should know something about it when you choose plants. Some, like azaleas and rhododendrons, thrive in acid soil. Others such as FILIPENDULA, Meadowsweet, and GYPSOPHILA, Baby's-breath, love sweet or limy soil. To sweeten an acid soil add lime; to reduce alkalinity add gypsum. Or to make acid soil add aluminum sulphate at half a pound per square yard (200 grams per square meter). To neutralize all soils, and this is where most plants are the happiest, add organic material such as compost, manure, humus or well-rotted leaves.

It may sound like too much trouble but in the long run soil improvement will reward you a thousand times over. When I stopped being impatient with my garden, I took one section

MECONOPSIS, *the famous Himalayan Blue Poppy, grows in an astonishing number of climate zones. It might be difficult in cold places but definitely worth trying down to **Zone 4.***

and worked on it for a year or two and then put it into production. Good soil became much better, more quickly.

Knowing about your soil can mean that you'll be able to grow surprising things. At the Devonian Botanical Garden in Edmonton they grow MECONOPSIS, Himalayan Blue Poppies, splendid ones, in an area where it's supposed to be too cold. It's a matter of soil content.

You probably have soil in your garden that is good enough to plant now. Divide your spaces into sections, use one part, and get on with improving the others. By the time you get back to the first section, you'll see what soil improvement does for the health of your plants.

BUMPING UP THE SOIL ❧ To bump up the soil, dig down two to three feet making trenches. In the bottom of each trench add compost, peat and humus. Break up the soil you took out and turn it over until it becomes friable or workable and put it back into the trench. Rake more organic material over the top. You can use this in a few weeks.

If the soil is really wretched put everything you've got—leaves, compost, manure (the bagged well-rotted kind) in it and leave for as long as you have patience. Turn the soil on a regular basis and keep adding organic matter. The day will come when you've got prize earthworms living out there and a rich dark brown loam. Turn it over, let it settle for a week or two, then get on with planting.

BUYING AND PLANTING NURSERY STOCK

The next step after planning and soil preparation is purchasing the actual plants. It sounds jolly to buy thousands of seeds, and set them out in egg cartons to germinate. But they take from six weeks to a few months to show any growth at all, unless you have a greenhouse, cold frames or gro-lights to give them an early start. You'll want some kind of instant gratification especially in the early years. Go to a nursery.

And find a good nursery. Not a supermarket for plants. Best of all is a grower—that's the place where you can see fields of plants outside—whose staff knows what they're selling and who're willing to take the time to tell you how to care for your plants. This is a big investment on both sides. Nursery stock is expensive and a good plantsperson will want you to come back season after season.

Never, ever walk into a nursery without a plant list in hand. For years I'd come home with the same stuff I bought the week before. And young plants are anonymous. They're sitting under gorgeous illustrations of their most perfect mature form. So seductive. Never trust the photographs. It may take two years before they look this good. And you might end up with something that doesn't even look like the picture at all. Increasingly I find that plants are not identified properly or the color is wrong. It's maddening.

Before, if you let me loose in a nursery I'd go crackers. I'd buy things because I was drawn to

Opposite: (Zone 5) Romulus and Sandra St Laurent's intimate city garden designed by Ruth Dynbort is a serene oasis. From the right: ARTEMISIA *'Silver Mound';* VERONICA SPICATA, *Speedwell;* ALCHEMILLA MOLLIS, *Lady's Mantle;* COREOPSIS; LYTHRUM *'Morden Pink'; Virginia Creeper;* BETULA PENDULA YOUNGII. *The urns hold* IMPATIENS *and* LOBELIA.

a color, or a name, or something I'd seen in another garden. It's fun to shop like this, you can indulge your passions. It just doesn't add up to a terribly coherent picture.

Make a list and try to stick to it. Then file in a safe place (more on that later) to keep track of what you've bought.

BUYING PERENNIALS

Choosing a plant is not as easy as you might think. Don't grab the first one because it's at the front of the lot. Be fussy. If you are drawn to one with lots of blooms and very tall, don't touch it. Unless, that is, you're a closet Florence Nightingale and love to nurse things along. It's too far gone and the shock of transplanting will probably kill it. Go for one that looks strong but not leggy. If it has one bud about to open at least you'll be certain of the color you're buying.

Take it home and plant it as soon as possible. Above all don't let it sit in a heated car for hours or languish out in the full sun. This is a fragile creature. If necessary, soak the plant until you have time to put it in the ground. Nursery stock ordered from catalogues should be plunged into a pail of tepid water for at least five or ten minutes before planting.

PRINCIPLES OF PLANTING

Plant early in the day or when it's slightly cloudy. Prepare the soil by digging the right size hole. A good rule of green thumbery is to make the hole a lot bigger than you think necessary. Mix the following into the soil at the bottom of the hole: well-moistened peat, a bit of manure, and bone meal—for acid-loving plants stick to the first two ingredients. Add some soil and water thoroughly. Then knock the plant

out of its little container: grasp the green stuff between your fingers, turn it upside down and give it a good bung on the side. It should come out fairly easily if it isn't totally potbound. In that case it may take a couple of hard whacks to get it out. If it's this difficult, cut out any roots that look sick or dead.

Water the hole again, put in the plant and fill in with soil, then tamp it down to expel any air holes. Plants need oxygen but not this way. Add more soil, tamp some more. Fill the whole thing in, then lean hard with the heel of your hand or shoe. Water once again. If you can, keep the plant shaded for a couple of days until it's adjusted to the new surroundings. Once the plant has taken root—you see the new growth appear—mulch it. Don't let the mulch actually touch the plant or it might get smothered. Don't mulch when the ground is wet or you'll lock in the moisture and end up with rotten crowns. And don't mulch bone dry soil either, or it will take the water too long to reach the roots where it's needed.

PLANTING SCHEDULE ❧ I tend to keep planting all summer, not just in the spring as is the tradition in many parts of North America. Because a perennial has to make half-decent roots before the onslaught of winter to survive, take this into account if you plan to buy or are given plants late in the season.

❧ Spring blooming plants should not be lifted or moved until after the flowers are finished.

❧ Fall blooming plants can be safely transplanted in spring.

❧ Always replant at exactly the same level the plants were originally. For example, peonies and irises thrive close to the surface.

❧ Plants with little rosettes, like SAXIFRAGA or SEMPERVIVUM TECTORUM, Hen-and-chickens, are easy to handle. Just pick out the best little offshoots and replace them at the same level.

DIVISION ❧ Divide spring-bloomers in fall in time for roots to retake before freeze-up; divide fall-bloomers in spring. Plants that grow in clumps must eventually be divided or the middle will die out from lack of nutrition and sunlight. Dig the plant up with your sharp garden spade and then pull it apart with your hands, the garden spade or a strong, sharp knife. Don't worry, you aren't going to kill it even though it may seem as if you're being singularly violent.

(Zone 9) Sybil McCulloch has many unusual plants in her garden including this variety of PAPAVER ORIENTALE, *Oriental Poppy.*

❧ To divide an old plant, take it apart in several clumps and choose whichever looks the healthiest; replant either in a new, well-prepared site or in the old site after it's been redug and bumped up again.

❧ Some plants hate being moved: ACONITUM, Monkshood; ASCLEPIAS TUBEROSA, Butterfly Plant or Weed; BAPTISIA, Wild Indigo; DICTAMNUS ALBUS, Gas Plant; EUPHORBIA, Spurge; GYPSOPHILA, Baby's-breath; HELLEBORUS NIGER, Christmas Rose; LIMONIUM, STATICE, Sea Lavender; PAPAVER ORIENTALE, Oriental Poppies; and THERMOPSIS, False Lupine.

❧ Some plants love to be divided: ACHILLEA, Yarrow; HOSTA, Plantain Lilies; HEMEROCALLIS, Daylilies; CHRYSANTHEMUM X SUPERBUM, Shasta daisies; MONARDA DIDYMA, Bee Balm.

LAYERED CUTTINGS ❧ You can encourage some plants to root by putting a stone or some dirt on one section of a low-growing stem or anything that will keep it in contact with the ground. Once it looks like the stem has developed new roots, tug at it gently and if it holds, slice the rooted part away from the mother plant and find this rooted cutting a new home.

PRINCIPLES OF PERENNIAL MAINTENANCE
I have one hort buddy who always has great clumps of plants to give away. She rips and tears away at her gorgeous garden. If I do that, I end up with a lot of corpses. I tend to be a lot more cautious. I use the planting trowel to lift out bits and pieces for filling in empty spaces or to pass along. It's hard to give plants away at first. You're always convinced that nothing will ever grow again. Don't worry. Be generous. Gardening is a bit like love, you have to give to get.

Don't let any plant intimidate you. They need good care but they aren't the fragile beauties they appear to be. They are quite tough and their will to survive is extraordinary. In fact, if a plant seems dead leave it alone for at least two years. There may be quiet action going on in the root system and you'll be surprised by a seemingly miraculous comeback. Once you've stopped being nervous about doing the wrong thing, you'll relax with the material you have to work with. It will do both you and the plant a lot of good.

On the whole, moving plants around is not only good for them but also good exercise for you. Gertrude Jekyll used to advise pulling up perennials and dividing them every year. She had nine gardeners. You probably just have you. With some exceptions divide them up and move them every two to three years. Plants with long tap roots don't want to be touched at all. And there are the exceptional ones that will take over your garden if you don't chop them up annually. These varieties will be pointed out in the plant Listings.

WATERING ❧ Watering is one of the most relaxing things you can do in your garden. Water deeply when the top 3 inches (7 centimeters) is dry and do it by hand if you can possibly take the time and have the patience. Some plants don't like to get their foliage wet, others don't like too much water and still others are what are known as gross feeders. This great term means they like lots of water and fertilizer. You will get to know your plants well. If you don't have the time, try one of the drip or soaker hose systems that water the ground rather than the foliage. As water becomes a scarce commodity, this will increasingly become the most sensible system to use. The politically correct garden is the garden of the future.

❧ NEVER water your garden at high noon. You run the risk of burning the foliage. It's absolutely wasteful since so much of the water evaporates. I find that the early morning before everyone else is about is my favorite time. I can stand around with a coffee and water whatever needs watering in peace and quiet. Don't water too late in the day and never after dark. Depending on the time of the year you probably shouldn't water after 6 p.m. If you do you run the risk of encouraging mildew to develop on some plants.

❧ Water deeply and not as often as you think you should. A light sprinkle will only encourage shallow roots that won't survive anything much at all and certainly not drought conditions. Deep watering means moisture will get down to below the root system and drain away easily. Test by putting a can beside the plant or border. When it has at least an inch in there, you've watered enough. If water sits

(Zone 9) Shirley Beach's rose collection evolved over almost 20 years. The rose illustrated is Easlea's Golden Rambler, underplanted with PAEONIA OFFICINALIS, *peony; left hand corner,* ALCHEMILLA MOLLIS, *Lady's Mantle;* GERANIUM SYLVATICUM *'Album', white geranium;* SILENE, *Catchfly; Dwarf* IRIS; PAEONIA, *unknown pink variety;* PAEONIA FESTIVA MAXIMA, *white peony flecked with crimson;* GERANIUM PRATENSE COERULEUM PLENUM, *Blue Geranium; and past the neighbor's lilac tree is a Bourbon Rose,* R. COMMANDANT BEAUREPAIRE (1874).

around on the surface, you have a drainage problem which has to be fixed. Rework the bed or the specific area in the bed.

DEADHEADING ❧ A garden filled with apparently dying plants is not a pretty sight. Deadheading isn't being finicky. Next to watering, it's one of the most important as well as relaxing, activities in the garden. You wander around snicking off spent blooms on both annuals and perennials before they can develop into seeds. All the plant's energy is programmed for its survival by setting seeds. If you take off the blooms as soon as they fade, the plant may flower again, and it will help encourage a strong root system and handsome foliage. You can nick old blossoms off with your fingers, bonsai scissors or secateurs. Make sure everything's clean. Do this any time of the day. It's another one of those wonderful tasks that makes you more intimate with the garden and with the shape and texture of your plants. Cut the stem back to the ground or to the nearest spot where a leaf is forming. A new stem and blossom may grow from the cut. Keep in mind that you can use deadheading to shape.the plant.

(Zone 5) Amy and Clare Stewart's garden has surprises running through it such as turning a corner and arriving at this gate. Left to right: LYCHNIS CHALCEDONICA, *Maltese Cross, the red plant beyond the gate; inside is a poppy and a lily about to burst into bloom; foreground shows* ARTEMISIA *by* OENOTHERA MISSOURENSIS, *Sundrops;* ANTHEMIS NOBILIS, *Roman chamomile;* CAMPANULA, *bellflower;* EREMUS, *Foxtail lily.*

SHEARING BACK ❧ Some plants, especially ground covers, really thrive when they are sheared back after blooming. Take off all the stems that have produced blossoms and leave only healthy foliage to either carry on looking good or to produce another batch of flowers. I've tried lots of experiments—cutting something right back to the ground, or just shaving off a little. Neither of these works particularly well. But if you grab a handful of spent blossoms and give your wrist a quick snap, you'll pull out any lifeless parts underneath as well as the dead flowers. You'll soon figure out for yourself what each plant needs. Special treatment for particular plants is mentioned in the Listings.

MULCH ❧ Mulch plants to hold in moisture and discourage weeds. This is like taking care of your own sensitive skin. To protect plants in winter remove any old mulch and add new after the ground has frozen. In spring remove it when the danger of frost is over and first growth starts to appear (see page 56 for lots more information).

KEEPING RECORDS ❧ Keeping a record of your garden is A Good Thing. It makes you feel very virtuous. Don't get suckered into one of those hideously expensive record books with lots of sections and ever-so-pretty. You want something that you can pick up and put down when you've got dirty hands. Get a loose-leaf binder with divisions that have pockets in which to shove in all the bills, plant lists and pieces of information you pick up from the nursery. This is where you put your shopping lists, keep track of what you buy, what you

plant, when you plant, and, if you can possibly remember, how it performs. One of the most enchanting diaries I have seen was simple notebooks kept by a gardener with pictures cut from seed packets and catalogues next to the record of performance over the years, when she'd divided and how well it responded.

You can stick an *aide-memoire* like a perpetual diary in your binder and record monthly instructions on what you should be doing in the garden. Keep tabs on the following information:

First Frost:
Last Frost:
Snow cover:
Hours of sunlight on certain dates:
Inches of rainfall:
What purchased; when planted; performance:

Another useful method of keeping tabs on your garden is making a map. A large piece of graph paper is good, or use the back of a poster as I did. Mark off the sections and indicate where you've put in new plants, how many, and their color. Here's where you can indulge in your need to use crayons or colored pencils but they aren't necessary. Make a plant list down one side. If you can't cope with this, and the necessity to change the list every time you put in new stuff, file the same information in the loose-leaf binder. Keep a file for each border.

The justification for this kind of work is that some plants are herbaceous—they die away in the winter time. You won't know what that thing is pushing up in the spring—weed or flower—if you don't know what and where you planted last year. A friend's father always said that if it came out easily it was probably a flower and if it came out with difficulty, it was probably a weed. "Probably" was the important part of that sentence. Unless you've got perfect recall you won't know which is which—another good reason to tag and map the garden.

By accumulating information about your garden you will be able to figure out its micro-climate. (See Your Microclimate, page 131.)

THE ECOLOGICAL GARDEN

The ecologically sound garden is the garden of the future. It employs the ancient practices of organic gardening. There are myriad reasons for being an organic gardener. You don't use chemicals and you do recycle all your organic detritus. You are self-sufficient. And you are making an effort to protect the environment. Most commercial chemical fertilizers dissolve so rapidly they end up reducing soil fertility. Then you're stuck with using more. Worst of all are herbicides which not only destroy weeds, but also kill off the earthworms and the result is poor soil. Doesn't seem terribly sensible to waste money on such stuff.

Once you stop waging chemical warfare against bugs, you may find a few new strangers coming in to eat. But that isn't nearly as terrible as helping deplete the ozone layer by using cans of dangerous sprays. There have been many experiments with non-toxic methods to get rid of the real pests. For every bug there is an enemy:

Aphids: lady beetles, midges, lacewings, damsel bugs

Slugs: rove beetles (they look like earwigs without the pincers); tiger beetles

Snails: fireflies eat snail, slug and insect larvae

Caterpillars: yellow jackets, hornets

Tent caterpillars: tachinid flies

You may not know what these things look like so put in the plants that attract them: lemon balm, thyme, dill, parsley; chives; Queen Anne's Lace (yes, some people think this is a weed but a few in the garden look handsome). Garlic will keep aphids, black spot away from your roses; chamomile attracts all sorts of beneficial bugs. Remember most bugs are our friends; don't treat them like the enemy.

Make your own traps: A commercial product like Tanglefoot spread on yellow plastic will attract winged aphids. A slug hotel is merely a container filled with beer and covered so it won't get diluted. These little muckers love to booze. Be sure to clean out the corpses every day. Slugs don't like anything gritty. Spread ashes or diatomaceous earth (see page 50) around to keep them at bay.

If you have the stomach, collect pests, put them into an old blender and swish them into a liquid diluted with water to spray on plants. The scent of death seems to be a deterrent.

Overall therapy: BT or Bacillus Thuringiensis is an organic compound which breaks down in sunlight so you have to reapply. It discourages earwigs and slugs. Plus try the following:

A steady stream of water from the hose will get rid of aphids. A bit of insecticidal soap (Safer's or any other biodegradable soap in the house), mixed in a solution and sprayed directly on the offensive beast helps. But you've got to make a direct hit to get results.

Collect cigarette butts and put them in a bottle with water and allow to ferment. This lethal solution dispatches an earwig in a second. If

Troughs are ideal for the high rise balcony garden. Fill them with low growing exotics such as SEMPERVIVUM, SEDUM, ECHEVERIA *and* LEWISIA.

Top and bottom left: (Zone 8) These troughs designed and grown by Don Armstrong indicate how extraordinary a few well-placed plants in a container can look. SAXIFRAGA; SEDUM; *and* LEWISIA COLUMBIANA.

Bottom right: (Zone 6) Shari Creed has an unusual combination of annuals, such as NIEREMBERGIA CAERULEA, *and the more exotic perennial Passion Flower vine in the pot with a tender fuschia underneath the silver leaf dogwood.*

nothing else it ought to put you off smoking. Entice them under rolled up newspapers, a board, an old umbrella left cunningly out at night. They love bedding down in lily trumpets. Then attack in the morning by shaking them out into the killer tobacco mix. It's hard to imagine hating a specific bug with passion, but once you've been bitten by an earwig you'll probably feel the same way.

Diatomaceous earth: this is ground up fossils, leftovers from prehistoric times—Fossil Flower Bug Killer contains it. This powder has a wide range of uses because it dries insects out. You can even use it on pets to kill fleas. Be careful. It attacks good and bad bugs alike.

I find it satisfying therapy to be out there on Slug Patrol in the early morning. Picking them off by hand and stomping on the loathsome beasts is a great way to rev up for a day in the competitive world. Except on the West Coast where their size, about that of small mice, is truly off-putting. These I'd suggest picking up by gloved hand and dispatching them into a large can of salt—shrivels them right up into nothing.

Leave some water out for the bugs to enjoy. If you have a little pond and can encourage a toad to take up residence you won't have any worries. A toad will keep your garden nice and clean. Make sure you leave some place for it to sleep in, to retreat to in winter—an overturned pot for instance—and that it has some protection from the local cat.

COMPOST

Composting is a method of putting back what you take out of the soil. It's called black gold by some more fanciful gardeners for good reason. Your soil is a living thing and like all living things needs to be fed properly. If you continue to take from it without returning anything, it dies. And though poor soil will support some plants, the majority won't like it much. Compost will improve lean soil slowly, making it healthy and friable.

HOW TO COMPOST

There's nothing particularly mysterious about composting—you simply put all your organic leftovers into a pile. They rot and eventually you have a crumbly black mixture of organic matter. This material helps to aerate the soil, enables it to absorb water and is, as well, an ideal mulch.

There are lots of fancy compost bins and composting appliances on the market. They are all probably pretty good. I've tried several but keep coming back to the following humble process: dig a hole and pile layers of green and brown debris in it: a layer of kitchen detritus, a layer of manure, then a layer of garden clippings cut in small pieces if they are twigs, then a layer of manure, then a layer of kitchen debris and so on using your common sense—keep layers of something green (garden clippings) followed by something brown (manure). Leave the pile somewhere out of sight, preferably where sun will hit it at some time during the day. Keep moist but not soggy and, if you're using lots of leaves, put some burlap on top held down with bricks or stone. Aerate it by leaving a piece of bamboo in the center and jiggling it around occasionally. Every few weeks turn the whole mess over. In a matter of months you'll have well-rotted material, and eventually you will have rich black stuff. This is compost—your mulch.

*(**Zone 5**) Midge Ellis Keeble installed broad wooden steps down into the ravine and her lower garden. From the bottom:* VERONICA SPICATA, *Speedwell;* SPIRAEA; ACHILLEA FILIPENDULA, *Yarrow;* ERIGERON, *Fleabane;* MALVA MOSCHATA, *Mallow.*

WHAT TO PUT IN THE COMPOST ❧ Leaves, green weeds—but not after they've gone to seed—lawn clippings uncontaminated by herbicides, plant leftovers; peat moss, which doesn't contain any minerals of its own, will help aerate the compost; tomato and squash vines, cornstalks, flower stems; kitchen stuff—if you have an old food processor or blender chop the leftovers before you toss them on the pile. This will speed up the decaying process. Add nut shells and coffee grounds with impunity. Then apply some blood meal, manure, cottonseed meal, rock phosphate, potash or other natural mineral fertilizers to give balance.

Keep in mind that a ton of compost occupies an area 4 x 4 x 4 feet (1.2 x 1.2 x 1.2 meters). You don't need a lot of space.

THE DO'S AND DON'TS OF COMPOSTING

DO: Ventilate. The bacteria essential to the breaking down of elements into compost need oxygen to perform. You can put a post or a pipe into your compost pile and wiggle it about or pull it out to allow air into the center. Or, you can buy something called a composting wand which will do much the same thing.

DO: Shred as much of your waste as possible; run a rotary mower back and forth over leaves and other garden detritus; or, along with a couple of neighbors, invest in a chipper/shredder. The finer the grind, the faster the fermentation and the eventual decaying process.

DO: Keep all material moist to start with by watering daily for three days.

DO: Turn the heap often—every three to four days.

DO: Add manure and other nitrogen-rich materials to speed up the process and to increase its nitrogen content.

DO: Keep it warm (therefore decaying) all

(Zone 9) George Radford designs each border with an eye to an overall sense of texture. HEMEROCALLIS; LAMIUM, *Lungwort;* SMILACINA RACEMOSA, *False Solomon's Seal are the background setting for a collection of* HOSTAS. *From left to right* H. LANCIFOLIA; H. FORTUNEI 'ALBOPICTA' H. UNDULATA 'ALBO-MARGINATA'.

winter by covering with burlap bags or soil.

DON'T: Make it of a single ingredient like leaves. It's the mix that counts; adding rich soil will help.

DON'T: Make it too big—you won't be able to turn the thing over or it may dry up.

DON'T: Add bones, fat or animal wastes—they attract animals, and won't break down quickly.

DON'T: Put in anything that's had chemicals added.

Finished compost is crumbly with a rich dark color. You may still see what's in it, but don't worry, it will break down in the final stages of decay around plants.

HOW TO USE COMPOST

Compost is so benign that you can even spread it around young plants. Put the compost through a coarse 2-inch (5-centimeter) sieve and throw anything bigger back into the pile to keep on breaking down. Turn soil and add compost to the top 4 inches (10 centimeters), put it on as heavily as you can or sift and bag for the future.

Use as follows:

Grass: Make sure it's finely ground.

Trees: Apply about a yard (just under a meter) away from the trunk.

Fall: Apply half-finished compost around plants in October and it will break down over the winter.

Spring: The ideal time of course. Add a mix of compost and bone meal to new beds and before you plant.

To make mulch, mix compost with topsoil for top or side dressing (that's when you add it to the top of the soil so you don't disturb the roots).

OTHER METHODS OF COMPOSTING

An elaborate method: Build two or three bins and move the compost from one to another as it ripens.

Cold rot: Throw stuff on the top and take it out of the bottom—make an enclosure 6 feet (2 meters) square by about 4 feet (1.2 meters) high with a space at the bottom large enough to get a spade in and remove the compost. Throw in everything mentioned above. In about six months to a year, you'll have a mix that's very rich in nitrogen.

A favorite of *Organic Gardening* magazine, the bible of organic gardeners:

14 DAY COMPOST ❧ To basic materials (anything biodegradable), add manure with a sprinkling of rock powder. Shred everything, mix and mound. If it hasn't heated up by the second or third day, add more dried blood meal to provide nitrogen. On the fourth day, turn heap, check temperature to make sure it's warming up, and add water if necessary. Seventh day, turn—pile should be cool. Tenth day, turn again; day 14, use. It's not fine humus but it will break down in the garden in a most satisfactory way.

SOIL IMPROVEMENT

To improve or change the quality of your soil, minerals are essential. Natural minerals work slowly, and won't burn young plants. As suggested earlier, try the following in each section of the garden: take a handful of moist soil and squeeze it. With all three soil types—sandy, clay, silt—add humus which will help bind the sandy soil and silt, and will aerate the clay soil. Peat moss, leaf mould, manure and, best of all, compost will correct your soil.

RAISED BEDS ❧ Raised beds can add another zone (see page 139) to your garden because the soil keeps warmer longer. With mulching you can experiment with all sorts of plants exotic to your area. Another bonus: if drainage is really bad in some areas of your garden, raised beds give you better control over moisture content and the quality of the soil.

The ideal, naturally, is to have a garden full of loam with perfectly balanced mineral content. Not many of us do, so work towards the ideal. Dig down a foot or so and add drainage material. It can be anything—leftovers from renovations, broken clay pots, pebbles—and then add improved soil to a minimum height of 10 inches (25 centimeters). Hold it up with wood siding, upright bricks or any other edging that looks attractive to you, and that keeps the soil from sliding onto paths when you water.

THE MINERAL CONTENT OF SOIL ❧ You may need to improve the mineral content of your soil. To determine this have it tested by the nearest Department of Agriculture. Send them soil samples from different parts of the garden, because it may vary from area to area. After you receive the results try the following:

For more nitrogen: Add dried blood or bone meal.

For more phosphorus (it improves production and does really well on acid soil): Add rock phosphate, bone meal.

For more potassium: Add manure and wood ashes, seaweed, kelp. Potassium is a major plant food and helps carry carbohydrates throughout the plant system, forms strong stems, fights disease, and reduces water requirements, essential to growth; helps plant utilize nitrogen. Use 20 pounds (9 kilograms) to 100 square feet (3 square meters).

Alkaline soil: The lower the rainfall, the more likely you are to have alkaline soil. To reduce alkalinity add peat moss and manure; to increase alkalinity add limestone.

Acid soil: Areas of very heavy rainfall tend towards acidity in the soil. If your soil is too acidic add limestone. If you need to increase acidity use peat moss specially designed for this purpose.

Whenever you are using peat moss in the loam-manure-peat moss mix, make sure it is well soaked or it will absorb the water needed by the soil. Start it off by pouring boiling water over the peat moss; and then let it sit for a week.

FERTILIZING

Fertilize before planting every year. Scratch fertilizer into the soil with a rake (or if you're starting a whole new section of garden, dig it in). If you add fertilizer as you plant, make sure it's deeper than the plant's roots so it's not touching them but available for easy feeding. You can also side or top dress by applying it near the plant during the growing season.

Fertilizers to use: manure (any well-rotted kind is good including mushroom manure with

(Zone 3) Margon Thiessen's river border shows the potential lushness of a prairie garden when it's located in a sheltered spot. From the front of the picture: RHEUM PALMATUM, *ornamental rhubarb;* JUNIPERUS *'Golden Pfitzer';* ARTEMISIA *'Silver Mound';* SEDUM KAMTSCHATICUM; *variegated* SEDUM *'Autumn Joy';* JUNIPERUS WILTONII; DIANTHUS DELTOIDES; GYPSOPHILA, *Baby's-breath.*

worm castings); blood meal, wood ash (potassium); bone meal (consists of calcium phosphate, phosphorus and nitrogen, but mostly phosphorus; use it with all but acid loving plants); superphosphate. Organic fertilizer available at good nurseries will list the contents on the package.

REVIVING THE SOIL

Since I've worked on my garden in sections, it's been relatively easy to revive the poor soil. After hauling away all the garbage we rented a rototiller, but digging is just as effective. What was most encouraging was to see worms. We knew the soil was salvageable. If you haven't got earthworms you haven't got the bacterial population you need for lively soil—beg or buy worms.

Start by digging in as much manure as you can afford along with some peat moss (about one third as much). Then let a year's supply of leaves and garden detritus lie fallow on the surface. The following year, rototill or dig in another supply of leaves, manure, peat, bone and blood meal. The worms will be gigantic and it's time to put the soil into production.

Earthworms are essential to your garden. Get to know them. They love to nest and hate to be moved. They work their way through the soil gobbling up everything in their path and excreting mineral-rich castings. One worm can produce its weight in castings every day and may go down six feet aerating your soil for you. They create a porous soil allowing water to work its way more easily through the soil. An earthworm will even draw leaves deep into the soil and break them up for you. They keep on fertilizing even after death. The humus you get from earthworm castings is incomparable. And it's bacterial action that creates humus. Worms can't abide strong chemicals. Chemicals kill the things you should love. If you think I feel strongly about not using chemicals, you are absolutely right.

MULCH

Whether you are an organic gardener or not, you should know something about mulch. This is organic matter you put on the soil to stop weeds, hold in moisture and improve the soil. Mulch protects plants during winter and reduces the hazards of freeze-thaw heaving. It keeps the stress level of the plant down. Stressed out plants don't grow beautiful blooms—not for long.

THE DO'S AND DON'TS OF MULCHING

DON'T: Mulch when there's been a lot of rain or the soil is water-logged. This can rot the plant.

DON'T: Mulch when the soil is too dry or you'll prevent rain from getting to the roots easily.

DON'T: Mulch boggy soil.

DON'T: Mulch seedlings immediately because mulch holds in humidity and can cause a fungus-like disease called damping-off.

DO: Mulch tender plants after the ground has frozen, for the best winter protection.

WHAT TO USE AS MULCH ❧ Compost of course is the best of all; and leaves (especially around acid-loving plants). Some, however, such as maple leaves can form a killer mat and end up suffocating the plants. Any leaves lying around in your garden will break down eventually, but it's better to use leaf mould—shredded leaves on their way through the decaying process. Hulls of cocoa beans are one of my favorites—they look good and they break down easily. Your garden will smell like a chocolate sundae for a few days but that will fade; or, newspaper with a layer of wood chips on top; stones and rocks of various grades are good-looking and will gently release minerals. For anyone living by the sea, salt straw from marshes, or seaweed and kelp are excellent; wood and bark chips—though I find them just a bit too institutional; clean straw if you're near a farm; sphagnum moss is good as is a mixture of weeds, native grasses mixed with grass clippings; presoaked peat moss mixed with manure and compost. Mushroom manure is excellent and has already been sterilized of all weed seeds. I am not a big fan of plastic mulching.

To make an *acid mulch* combine peat moss with manure and good soil. Allow lumps to freeze and crumble all winter then apply in spring.

How much: a thin layer of finely shredded material is more effective than unshredded loose stuff. Go as thick as three inches if you have enough material. I never do.

FINDING INTERESTING PLANTS

When you first start to invest in perennials you'll buy what's available at the most convenient place, whether it's the corner grocery store or a local nursery. But you'll soon get tired of what they have to offer. It's much more fun to find plants that everyone on the street doesn't have. Your plant base and theirs too will expand when you start dividing them up and passing them around.

There are a number of sources for good plants, such as regional seed houses where you can be sure everything will be hardy to your area; and catalogues from houses that ship both live plants and seeds. The latter usually offer new varieties to tempt you and most of them ship all over the country. Some charge for their catalogues but most don't.

GARDEN SOCIETIES

One of the reasons I started gardening was because I could do it alone. I'm not much of a joiner, but one of the biggest favors you can do for yourself as a new gardener is to join different societies. Just because you are a novice doesn't mean you should be shy about talking to experienced gardeners. Gardeners are the least intimidating people to meet, most of them are not only friendly but eager to share their knowledge. Many societies have seed exchanges and lists of nurseries that specialize in certain kinds of plants. I've found joining rock garden and native plant societies a huge bonus, and I receive regular bulletins which are well-written and endlessly fascinating. It doesn't matter whether or not you have a rock or a wild garden, the point is to keep educating yourself.

If you become interested in a certain family of plants, however arcane your interest, there is a society somewhere in North America that shares your enthusiasm. It's through these adventurous gardeners that you'll find your most exotic plants.

Find the nearest botanical garden and see if they have a plant introduction society. They provide plants that can be grown in your area with great success.

TALKING IN THE GARDEN

It may sound pretentious to hear Latin run trippingly off the tongue of an experienced gardener. It's not. There's a very good reason for knowing some botanical Latin. Let's take the case of Dusty Miller. This is a common plant with grey foliage. Looks nice in the border. Adds a different kind of texture to all that green. But the name Dusty Miller can be variously applied to SENECIO MARITIMA, ARTEMISIA STELLERANA or CENTAUREA GYMNOCARPA. They sort of look alike but they are different plants with different needs.

If you despair because you can't remember all those names, take courage. Russell Page, one of the great garden designers of this century, admitted that he had a tough time remembering the botanical name of any given plant unless he'd written it down dozens of times. There is hope for the rest of us.

The other case for learning some botanical Latin is that if you become an obsessive gardener, you'll want to look at gardens wherever you go. Botanical Latin is the universal language used to describe plants. Even if it takes a couple of years to feel at ease saying a lot of this stuff out loud, you won't regret it.

For instance there is comfort in knowing that whenever you see a plant described as ALBA you know it's white, or FLORE-PLENO you know it has multiple blooms. Here's a starter list of one hundred basic botanical Latin terms.

Plants are always listed by the genus (pl. genera), followed by species, then by variety, for example: AQUILEGIA (genus), FLABELLATA (species), ALBA (variety).

If the variety (the third word) is named after a famous botanist or place you'll know a bit about the plant. For instance, anything with Margery Fish's name on it is probably a shade plant—she's the big expert in the field. Later, the history and background of plants will interest you more. But now concentrate on the basics. If the genus is mentioned the second time in a text it will be capitalized as a single letter; the species spelled out, ARTEMISIA LUDOVICIANA, A. LACTIFLORA.

Pronunciation (we've put a guide in with the plant Listings) doesn't matter (though heaven knows some gardeners can be snobs about it). Other things you should know:

Binomial: Two names, the first is the genus and a noun; the second is the species (usually descriptive) and an adjective. The ending must agree (masculine, -us; feminine, -a; neuter, -um). Greek has neuters ending in -on; but some like RHODODENDRON, PENSTEMON are masculine; Greek feminine, -as, -e, -es, -ex, -is, -s, -ys.

RHIZO means root.

PHYLLON and FOLIUM indicate the leaf.

ANTHOS is the flower.

CARPUS means fruit.

Numbers: NUI, MONO—one; BI, DI—two; TRI—three, and so on through QUIDRI, TETRA, PENTA, OCTO. For example, TRICHOPHYLLUM means a leaf in three parts.

-OIDES means like: BRIOIDES like a BRIOPHYTE or moss-like.

Sometimes plants are named after the person who discovered them in the wild or in commemoration of a famous horticulturist. An -A ending is commemorative (LINNAEA after Carolus Linnaeus, the great 18th century botanist; or LEWISIA for Meriwether Lewis of the Lewis & Clark expedition); -I indicates the discoverer of the plant (DOUGLASI after David Douglas, a famous plant explorer of the 19th century especially on the West coast; HOOKERI after William or Joseph Hooker).

ADUNCA: hooked

AFFINIS: related or similar to

AGGREGATA: clustered

ALBIFLORUM: white-flowered

ALNIFOLIA: alderlike foliage

ALPINA\ALPESTRIS\ALPINUM: alpine\higher up\even higher

ANGUSTIFOLIUM: narrow leaved

ARENA: sand

ARGENTEA: silvery

ARGUTA: toothed

ATROPURPUREA: very purple

AURANTIACUS: orange

AUREUM: golden

BREVIFOLIA: short-leaved

CAESPITOSA: growing in tufts

CAMPANULATUS: bell-shaped

CAMPESTRIS: of the fields

CANESCENS: hoary-surfaced

CARDINALIS: scarlet

CAUDATUM: tailed

CAULESCENS: having a stem

CEREUM: waxy

CERNUUM: drooping

CERULEA: blue

CITRINUM: lemon colored

COMPOSITUS: clustered

CONTORTA: twisted

CORDIFOLIA: heart-shaped leaf

CORNUTA: horned or hornlike

CORONARIA: forming a crown

CRASSIFOLIUS: thick-leaved

CYANEUS: blue

DENTATUM: toothed

DIFFUSA: spreading

DIVERSIFOLIA: of different leaves

ECHINOIDES: prickly

ELATUM: tall

ELEGANS: graceful

FAVESCENS: yellowish

FLORIBUNDA: free flowering

FORMOSA: beautiful

FRAGILIS: brittle

FRUTESCENS: shrubby

GLABRUM: smooth

GLAUCA: grey or bluish

GRACILLIMA: very slender

GYPSOPHILA: loves gypsum or a limy soil

INCANA: greyish hue

LACTEUS: milky white

LANATUM: woolly, soft, hairy

LANCEOLATA: lance or spear-shaped

LANUGINOSA: woolly

LATIFOLIA: broad-leaved

LITTORALIS: grows by seashore

LONGIFLORA: elongated flower

LONGIFOLIA: long-leaved

LUTEUM: yellow

MARGARITACEA: pearly

MARITIMUM: growing by the sea

MILLEFOLIUM: thousand-leaved

MONTANUS: of the mountains

MULTIFLORA: many flowered

NANUM: small, dwarf

NEMOROSA: lives in shady places

NIVALIS: of the snow

PALUSTRIS: growing in marshy ground

PANICULATUS: flowers in a panicle

PATULA: spreading

PENTANDRA: five stamens

PERENNIS: perennial

PETIOLATUM: with a leaf stalk

PLICATA: folded or pleated

POLYACANTHA: many spines

POLYPHYLLA: many-leaved

PROCUMBENS: lying flat on the ground

PUMILUS: low, or small

PUNCTATUS: dotted

PUNGENS: sharp-pointed

RACEMOSUS: flowers singly along a stem

RAMOSA: branching

REPENS: prostrate, creeping

RUBRA: red

SCABRELLA: somewhat rough

SEMPERVIVUM: evergreen

SERRATUS: saw-toothed

SPECIOSA: showy

SPECTABILIS: spectacular

SPINESCENS: spiny

STELLATA: starlike

STOLONFERAL: producing runners or stolons

STRIATUS: long lines

TOMENTELLA: somewhat hairy

VENENOSUS: poisonous

VENUSTA: graceful

VESCA: feeble

VISCIDA: sticky

VULGARA: common

And of course many plants are identified from their home: CANADENSIS, from Canada; JAPONICA, from Japan; CALIFORNICA, from California. Remembering these 100 terms is like beginning to learn a new language and stretching your mind. Neither can hurt.

GARDEN VARIATIONS

*T*here are many styles of gardens that can be established anywhere in the country and in any zone. What follows are a few of them along with illustrations of what some clever gardeners have done with their sites.

BULBS IN THE GARDEN

Of course you'll want to have bulbs in your garden. There's nothing quite like them for a good early spring show. Plant them in the most casual way possible. Follow the usual rule—never, ever plant in rows or rigid geometric patterns. This is another of those public garden excesses to avoid at all costs. If you still have grass you can plant bulbs in drifts through the grass and then wait until all the stems have turned brown or ripened (that's next year's food) before you mow the grass. Or group them together in tens and twenties to form clumps.

I gently roll my bulbs out of a basket to see where they might like to rest to get an idea for the shape of the clump. If you want a succession of blooms, plant bulbs of the same species at different depths. Try planting bulbs under shrubs and large plants such as peonies. You have to be a little careful here—keep about 12 inches (30 centimeters) away from the root system.

My favorite bulbs: Species Tulips (TULIPA TARDA; T. KAUFMANNIANA); NARCISSI (especially POETAZ and TRIANDRUS); FRITILLARIA (F. IMPERIALIS, Crown Imperial or Skunk Lily, is a huge beast; but F. MELEAGRIS is a small mysterious creature that looks good anywhere); MUSCARI—the little grape hyacinths that bear no resemblance to the coarse things sold in pots—hundreds of them, you can't have too many of these or of SCILLA, commonly known as squill or Siberian bluebells; ALLIUM of all kinds to be planted among taller perennials; IXIOLIRION, Lily-of-the-Altai; CHIONODOXA, Glory-of-the-snow.

ON PLANTING BULBS ❧ Most bulbs need to be planted in the fall. They want a head start before the first frost but some of them can be put in right up to freezing time (just make sure you've got all the holes prepared before then). The old rule of thumb is to plant a bulb three times its thickness deep. They are usually accompanied by instructions. Follow them carefully. Make a hole, scratch in Bulbooster or bone meal first. Water. Place the bulb pointed side up. Water. Fill in the hole and scatter bone meal on the surface. Water again.

Bulb Pests: Squirrels are the bane of my gardening life. We are at constant war especially during the fall when bulbs should be planted. If you plant tulips, which they adore, around FRITILLARIA, Crown Imperial, which they hate, you may actually get some survivors. Companion plant—narcissi and daffodils are both poison to the little beasts so put them near the succulent lilies and tulips they love to eat. Plant moth balls along with the bulbs; blood meal

(Zone 6) FRITILLARIA MELEAGRIS, *Snakes' Head, is a strangely beautiful bulb that comes from the wild and shows its mysteries in spring.*

*(**Zone 5**) Bill and Lynne Aimers have many borders of spring blooming bulbs. This shows how felicitous a display groups of similar tulips can make.*

*Opposite: (**Zone 6**) One of Ellen Eisenberg's great passions is collecting bulbs. This is a partial look at what putting in hundreds of bulbs each year can accomplish. She groups them in clumps of at least a dozen to achieve this splendid array.*

sprinkled over the surface after you've planted is not only good for the bulbs but the smell of death can discourage most rodents. On the other hand it could make a dog frenetic or even sick. Reapply after watering. A sprinkle of cayenne pepper on the surface after every rain will also discourage animals.

GOING NATIVE: THE NATURAL GARDEN

In times of rapid climate changes, the most sensible things to introduce into your garden are native plants. As the name implies, these are species that have been here, developing and adapting, since the last Ice Age 10,000 years ago. Species grown in the wild for eons will be the hardiest you can find. There are also relative newcomers which came across on the ships of the first settlers. We now accept these familiar interlopers as an integral part of our landscape and almost as natives.

Some of these plants you may think of as weeds. But as horticulturists say, "One man's weed is another man's favorite garden plant." Beauty here is truly in the eye of the beholder. For instance, I happen to have a few SOLIDAGO, Goldenrod, in my garden. I love the rich yellow of this particular species. It does not cause allergenic reactions—that's ragweed.

I also have a few specimens of DAUCUS CAROTA, Queen Anne's Lace, coming along nicely. They were deposited by a bird or from seed stuck to the bottom of my walking shoes. Although a bit surprised by their presence, they've become a welcome addition to the garden.

Natural gardening then is an extension of the idea that you can bring the surrounding countryside into your backyard and come up with surprising and wonderful results. You will also have a garden that requires less maintenance since these creatures have survived on their own for so long. No hybrid fragility here, unless they've been bred from the wild to be hardier for specific circumstances such as drought.

If you designate just one part of your garden as native and choose the right plants for the site, you'll not only cut down on your own labor but also reduce the need for watering.

A word of caution about collecting native plants. Buy only from nurseries that breed them; who aren't ripping them out of the wilderness and destroying part of the environment. Grow from seed bought from Aimers' Wildflowers and other respectable seed companies. If you see an area about to be assaulted by heavy machinery save any plants you can; collect them from the sides of railways; but don't take them out of parks and recreation areas.

Use plants indigenous to your region of the country. Look at them in the wild or in their natural habitat. They will give you clues about what they need: grey leaves mean they require sun; great big dark green leaves say that they can take shade. They will all probably require well-drained soils. That's loose soil with some sand content. You won't have to worry so much

(Zone 5) Jeanne Marler's enchanting little border has an ethereal quality.
FESTUCA GLAUCA OVINA, Blue Sheep's Grass, is combined with GYPSOPHILA, Baby's-breath;
a single white PAEONIA, peony; and a lily.
The intense yellow of the annual marigolds is a striking contrast.

about fertilizing your wildlings once they're established. By adding compost, they'll get along even better with you than they did in their original home.

You'll want to get rid of as much grass as you can—again a stroke that will cut down on your work like crazy. As I mentioned, I did this years ago and it has been far more liberating than I can successfully describe. No machines are taking up space for one thing. I find it much more interesting to walk around on ground cover pulling out the occasional weed than mowing lawns. But then I don't have a high volume of traffic in my garden. If you do, you'll probably have to be content to have some grass, but isolate it to pathways or areas where there will be a lot of activity. Make it just one element of your design rather than the central focus.

If you think of the Earth as having a skin, well, part of a plant's function is to protect that

(Zone 8) Kathie Leishmann has a true designer's eye.
Whenever she installs a new combination of plants she not only keeps a sense of harmonious color,
but also the textures of each plant. Left to right: HUMULUS LUPULUS *'Aureus', yellow-leaved form of hops;*
LUNARIA REDEVIVA, *Honesty;* KERRIA JAPONICA *'Variegata';* VIBURNUM TINUS; ARTEMISIA LUDOVICIANA;
MILIUM EFFUSUM *'Aureum', Bowles' Golden Grass;* LILIUM; *in front, a species contoneaster.*

*(**Zone 5**) Lambert De Wit adds pink to complement the yellows and silvers in this border:*
AJUGA VARIEGATA; ECHINOPS, *Globe Thistle;* ACHILLEA FILIPENDULA; HELIANTHUS, *small sunflower;*
SPARTINA PECTINATA 'AUREA-MARGINATA' *'Prairie Cord Grass';*
SENECIO ADONIFOLIUS; SAXIFRAGA PELTORPHAGIN.

skin. If you don't keep your soil covered up, weeds will perform that service for you. Plants prevent the sun from scorching the soil and turning it into dust or sand. Ground covers, anything that crawls along or hugs the ground, operate much the same way that mulch does—they protect the soil, suppress weeds, and hold in moisture.

Some ground covers will flourish with very little sun and water: HEDERA HELIX, English Ivy; PACHYSANDRA TERMINALIS, Japanese Spurge;

VINCA MINOR, Periwinkle; AJUGA REPTANS, Bugleweed; and EPIMEDIUM, Barrenwort, which is one of the most satisfying ground covers of all. These are the lowest of low maintenance plants. For a sunnier area try as many THYMUS, Thymes, as you can find. You can create a tapestry effect with the wide variety of textures and colors available in this wonderful species.

To get ideas for your wild garden, study any in your neighborhood or visit conservation areas to get a grip on what will grow most successfully.

(Zone 5) ECHINOPS, *Globe Thistle, is a fine*
architectural plant used here in
Lambert De Wit's garden with other plants that
come into bloom in July and August.

To the left: (Zone 5) Lambert De Wit utilizes
native plants through his vast garden in
well orchestrated plantings. LYTHRUM *naturalizes*
wonderfully in the background.
In the foreground the combination of Ribbon grass
and deep purple SALVIA X SUPERBA *contrasts with*
ACHILLEA FILIPENDULA *'Gold Plate' and*
A. *Cerise Queen.* CIMICIFUGA, *another native plant,*
has white spires next to the glaucous grass.
The large plant is RUDBECKIA LACINIATA.

CREATING A MEADOW

Almost any type of soil is suitable for a meadow as long as it's well-drained and isn't too rich. At least six hours of sun must hit the spot you've designated. You can buy wildflower seeds by the pound but be sure and include annuals in the mix. It will take about two years for the perennials to grab hold and bloom. Walks could be paths mowed through it. Prepare as you would for a lawn—dig it up, water, let it settle (See The Soil, page 39). Mix seeds with horticultural sand if they are tiny. Broadcast; rake lightly with soil and spray with water. Give a good soaking twice a week for a month. Once established, your meadow won't need watering except in drought. Mow it in August or wait until fall for seeds to ripen. Leave a thin layer of cuttings on the ground as mulch.

If your garden is in such a virgin state you think it's covered with weeds, you may have the start of a natural garden already. In all that dross there is probably gold. Let it continue to grow and pluck out anything that you don't like; isolate the plants that appeal to you and let them thrive without competition.

Add some of the things you favor from the native plants in Listings. RUDBECKIA FULGIDA 'Goldsturm,' Black-eyed Susan, or HEMEROCALLIS, Daylily, in any color make a good start. Create little islands in what seems to be the surrounding confusion. LYTHRUM SALICARIA, Purple Loosestrife, may be too large in an ordinary border but look perfect at the edge of a meadow; the native North American aster and all its varieties will fit in comfortably. Grasses of course come into their own in the well-thought-out meadow.

Be sure to pull out dandelions, crab grass and noxious creatures such as bindweed. This is the stuff that looks like a dwarf morning glory. In fact it is POLYGONUM CONVULVUS. And it is deadly. It will strangle everything in a few years. So don't be tempted by its pretty little flowers.

Meadowland plants: ASCLEPIAS, Butterfly Weed; COREOPSIS, Coreopsis; COSMOS; DAUCUS CAROTA, Queen Anne's Lace; ECHINACEA PURPUREA, Purple Coneflower; ESCHSCHOLZIA CALIFORNICA, California Poppy; EUPATORIUM MACULATUM, Joe-pye Weed; HEMEROCALLIS, Daylily; LIATRIS, Gay Feather or Blazing Star; LYSIMACHIA, Loosestrife; MACLEAYA CORDATA, Plume Poppy; SOLIDAGO, Goldenrod.

The range is so enormous that you have only to go over the listings under "Origin - North America" to find ones you'll be happy with. Summer is the time to forage around the countryside looking for plants that please you and that might transplant well into the garden. Or

(Zone 5) CHRYSANTHEMUM X SUPERBUM, *Shasta Daisy, is one of the most useful of all the border plants. Good cutting plant.*

wait until fall to collect seeds. Do this by covering seed heads with a small paper bag and shaking. Keep them in a cool place until you're ready to sow.

Take what's called vegetative cuttings through July and August—pull short twigs off at the base for a heel cutting and trim with a sharp knife. Trim off a little bark and put the cutting into a rooting mixture of sand and peat, or vermiculite and peat. Keep moist until roots develop.

Ornamental grasses will extend the length of the seasons well into fall and some even look handsome in winter. Their lovely arching forms belie their ease of cultivation. They are just about pest-free. You merely have to keep them in check if they start spreading too wildly. FESTUCA OVINA GLAUCA, Blue Fescue; and PENNISETUM ALOPECUROIDES, Fountain Grass, are superb.

Vines: CAMPSIS RADICANS, Trumpet Vine; PARTHENOCISSUS QUINQUEFOLIA, Virginia Creeper; PARTHENOCISSUS TRICUSPIDATA, Boston Ivy (not really a native but it serves as well); CELASTRUS SCANDENS, Bittersweet.

Winter trees: BETULA PENDULA, Weeping Birch, and any of the coniferous trees which keep their needles all year look attractive in the natural garden.

Shrubs: RHUS TYPHINA, Sumac; AMELANCHIER CANADENSIS, Serviceberry or Shadblow depending on what part of the country you live in.

A WOODLAND GARDEN

If you have some decent shade you might want to experiment with a woodland section in the garden. Many woodland plants like an acid soil and if you don't already have it you'll have to make it. Excavate the soil to about 12 inches

(Zone 4) AQUILEGIA, *Columbine. There are a hundred species of this delicate but extremely hardy perennial. Even when the blooms have left, the fernlike leaves give pleasure.*

(30 centimeters), add a layer of granulated peat mixed with cottonseed meal, top this off with a thin layer of superphosphate, and dig them in together. Epsom salts mixed with the subsoil will also help lower the pH. This will create moderately acid subsoil. Combine organic material such as humus, compost, manure and superphosphate with the topsoil. Then add more of the original soil and organic material; followed by a layer of superphosphate and ammonium sulphate. Dig this into the upper layer. The acid level in the soil will last about two years and then you will have to amend it. You can also temporarily change the pH around specific plants by doing the following:

To increase acidity: Add 1/2 cup (115 mL) of superphosphate to 1 gallon (4.5 L) of water. Or remove ground litter and sprinkle equal parts of powdered sulfur and ammonium sulphate on the ground over the roots. Replace the litter. Use an acid mulch in winter—either pine needles or compost you've made from sphagnum peat moss and soil that has over-wintered. Earthworms are alkaline-lovers and they won't be in your compost or your soil if it is acid. If you've got worms you've got neutral or sweet soil. You'll have to add more of the above ingredients to get the mix right.

To decrease acidity: water with a solution of garden lime—1/2 cup (115 mL) of lime to 1 gallon (4.5 L) water. Sprinkle lime around the plant under the ground litter. Or add limestone and bone meal when you are digging a hole for new plants.

If all this sounds too much like being a scientist rather than a gardener, make sure you know what your soil is like and choose your plants to fit the soil. This is probably one of the most important decisions you'll make.

Woodland Plants: ARISAEMA, Jack-in-the-pulpit; SYMPLOCARPUS, Skunk-cabbage; TRADESCANTIA VIRGINIANA, Spiderwort or Spiderlily; ERYTHRONIUM DENS-CANIS, Dog's Tooth Violet; SMILACINA RACEMOSA, False Solomon's Seal; TRILLIUM GRANDIFLORUM; CYPRIPEDIUM, Lady's Slipper; ASARUM CANADENSE, Wild Ginger; HEPATICA; AQUILEGIA CANADENSIS, Wild Columbine. There are hundreds of others to explore.

THE COTTAGE GARDEN

A cottage garden these days isn't what Gertrude Jekyll had in mind. It's more likely to be a garden at the cottage with most of the work accomplished in only two days a week. I have a friend who crawls around in the dark with a flashlight every Friday night figuring out what's to be done the next day. He swears he's going to buy a miner's lamp so he can more easily inspect and see how his garden has survived without him for the past five days. He isn't so much crazy as obsessed.

Gardening on the weekends carries its own pleasures and sorrows. The latter in not having access whenever you feel like stepping outside for a few moments of deadheading or pruning. On the other hand it imposes a certain discipline. You can't, by the nature of the beast, turn into a person who spends every waking hour out there in the garden.

To begin with, you have to plant extremely carefully. Planning and an intimate knowledge of your site are your two best assets. Ripping out great chunks of scenery to install grass that has to be manicured every weekend isn't necessarily an answer. But if you decide a garden isn't a garden without grass, be sure that you don't add lethal chemicals. They will leach through the soil into any nearby water damaging what you hope is your bit of wilderness.

(Zone 5) Tim Saunders uses native plants in careful combination with more domesticated varieties: Hardy Blue GERANIUM; ARTEMISIA ABSINTHIUM; PETUNIA; LOBELIA *'Crystal Palace'; 'Wild' daisies;* IBERIS; THYMUS MONTANA ALBUM; STACHYS BYZANTINA; MONARDA DIDYMA; GERANIUM SANGUINEUM ALBUM; HEMEROCALLIS; ARTEMISIA *'Silver King'.*

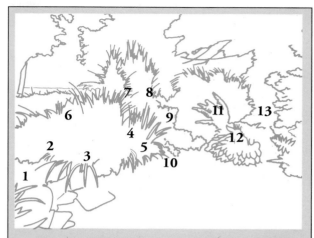

(Zone 5) Tim Saunders uses all of his cottage property, including the edge of the lake as potential garden beds:

1. GENTIANA ANDREWSII, *Closed Gentian*
2. IRIS VERSACOLOR, *Blue Flag Iris*
3. HOSTA UNDULATA *'Variegata'*
4. IRIS PSEUDACORUS, *wild iris*
5. HEMEROCALLIS *'Hyperion'*
6. IRIS SIBIRICA, *Blue Siberian Iris*
7. MISCANTHUS SINENSIS *'Variegatus'*
8. MISCANTHUS SINENSIS
9. SEDUM SPECTABILE
10. *an unidentified wild sedum found by the shore*
11. MATTEUCCIA STRUTHIOPTERIS, *Ostrich Fern*
12. HOSTA UNDULATA *'Albo-marginata'*
13. PHALARIS ARUNDINACEA *'Picta'*

Here's what photographer Tim Saunders did to make his weekend garden so satisfying. Grass, already growing, was about two-thirds weed which didn't bother him a bit. It's ground cover; gets cut every few weeks during the season and it doesn't demand any special care. He spent two seasons just looking at what would grow on his property and by canoeing around the lake observing what thrived in similar situations.

The idea was to let all the natural stuff in the garden flourish on its own, introduce more native plants, and add in other perennials that looked well with what was already there—in other words—to harmonize with each other.

With the help of wildflower books, Tim started identifying what surrounded him. He began to collect, very carefully, the wildlings that seemed to be most prolific. These are obviously the hardiest. They also have a reputation for being finicky about being moved. They proved, however, to be successful transplants.

Taking plants from the wild may be dicey. You should only touch places that have plenty growing and never take very much. Always leave a stand of wildflowers looking pristine. And never take anything without asking an owner's permission. It may be a wildflower garden you are disturbing.

Tim found an astonishing variety on his own property: blue, white and yellow violets; TRILLIUM; SANGUINARIA CANADENSIS, Bloodroot; HEPATICA; several kinds of fern; CHRYSANTHEMUM ROBERTIAM, Herb Robert; ASTER, Michaelmas Daisies; SAPONARIA OFFICINALIS, Bouncing Bet; wild NEPETA or Catmint; IRIS VERSICOLOR, Iris, Flag, native irises both blue and yellow; GENTIANA ANDREWSII, Closed Gentian; CHELONE, Turtlehead; MONARDA, Wild Bergamot; ASCLEPIAS, Milkweed; EUPATORIUM PURPUREUM, Joe-pye Weed.

Along the shore of the lake he had a plant that looked a bit like hosta. By cutting back the things growing around it, he made that stretch into a focal point. He calls it selective clipping. It goes in stages: let something go if it looks good; when it gets invasive, it's nipped into submission or is made into a feature on its own by removing other growth away from the main plants.

In the acidy soil and deep shade that covers most of his land, Tim introduced the following: MERTENSIA VIRGINICA, Virginia Bluebells; ASARUM CANADENSIS, Wild Ginger; VINCA MINOR, Periwinkle; PACHYSANDRA TERMINALIS, Spurge; BRUNNERA MACROPHYLLA, Siberian Bugloss; GALIUM ODORATUM, Sweet Woodruff; LAMIUM, Deadnettle; several kinds of hostas; PULMONARIA, Lungwort; and ferns.

In a particularly difficult area near trees whose aggressive root systems made working the ground almost impossible, he planted SEDUM TELEPHIUM, 'Autumn Joy', wild irises and daylilies. Native grasses serve as a backdrop. This mix of cultivated and wild plants all works with a singular kind of grace.

For spring he plants only narcissi, daffodils, scilla, and crocus. Tulips don't look right in a country garden he feels and, of course, they attract animals.

With a framework like this to work within, matching site with site when moving native plants around, Tim slowly added domesticated plants. He created special beds with good earth—topsoil, compost, manure and fertilizer for the first two years, maintaining them ever since with regular composting. These beds abut

*(**Zone 3**) L.G. Thomas's cottage garden was rescued from the nearby lake.*
Steps lead upwards to the cottage. SEDUM KAMTSCHATICUM, *Evergreen sedum;* BERGENIA CORDIFOLIA,
Heartleaf Bergenia; SAXIFRAGA UMBROSA, *London Pride are among the plants here.*

the wild areas which are kept under careful control. He uses specific plants such as hosta or ferns to act as a division between the cultivated bed and the native beds. But the aim is that the area must look like a garden.

In formal beds he has formal plants: Peonies which require no care; the true GERANIUM, Cranesbill—everywhere. In the shade they tend not to flower, but they are good foliage plants, and in sunnier spots they will come back with deadheading. VERONICA INCANA, Woolly Speedwell, and STACHYS LANATA, Lamb's-ears, both do well; variegated AJUGA, Bugleweed; CLEMATIS, Clematis; NEPETA FAASSENII, Catmint; ALTHEA, Hollyhocks; OENOTHERA,

Evening Primrose; PHLOX SUBULATA, Creeping Phlox; and hedges of ALCHEMILLA VULGARIS, Lady's-mantle, one of his favorite plants. He uses all kinds of DIANTHUS, Pinks, from low, creeping varieties to the elegant upright ones—mainly for the lovely grey foliage. Various kinds of very tailored ARTEMISIA are planted in the same bed with striking results. Astilbes and hostas are interspersed among wild things as though they'd always lived there.

In this garden the formal beds are in the foreground, beyond them ferns act as a background and a transition to native shrubs. They harmonize with the tone of the whole garden—muted, soft, elegant.

Keep things simple in a weekend garden; look for low maintenance plants and think in terms of broad strokes—great swathes of daylilies, for example, in mixed colors. If you clean up around the shrubs already on your land, you'll find that they become something special. Putting in a good ground cover like EPIMEDIUM, Barrenwort, or GALAX, underneath will hold back the weeds that will automatically spring up wherever you've been working.

Like any garden, no matter how hard you try, it isn't going to be maintenance-free. That's a fantasy. You're going to have to do some weeding and some watering, but you probably won't end up being tied to the garden if you start off with a good plan. But what's the point of having a garden if you aren't in it working?

THE FOLIAGE GARDEN

Foliage is a prime consideration when you design your garden. Sometimes it's hard to think beyond your favorite colors or color harmonies.

When you consider that your garden is going to be in foliage most of the time, it is foolhardy to ignore this most extraordinary part of a plant. Foliage is, of course, the skeleton of your garden. It's what anchors the design and gives it an understructure and substance.

Look at gardens designed with mainly foliage in mind. I've seen some so well-chosen, so balanced that my heart speeded up just being there. The sheer sensuality makes you want to reach out and touch.

Christopher Lloyd's definition of the perfect foliage plant is "One whose leaves are ornamental...and of greater aesthetic importance to the gardener than the flowers." The flowers may attract you as well, but you are looking beyond their brief glory.

The role of foliage plants in your garden is usually to give form to a bed or to use them on their own as accents. You can't shove them into a border with a scattergun approach. Using foliage properly is a very sophisticated approach to garden design. And by emphasizing the foliage, you'll have interest all year.

One of the garden gurus told a story on herself about the perfect plant. She'd read about it in an English gardening book—it had the legendary year-round interest from a deep scarlet in fall, to dull burgundy in early spring then a burst of life in shiny green with scented yellow flowers in late spring, blue berries in summer. With great difficulty she tracked down someone who could tell her where to find this paragon. "Ah," said the source, "it's growing all over your garden—that's MAHONIA AQUIFOLIUM." It is a native from Oregon with leaves that look a bit like holly. Somewhere in here there's a message about looking carefully at what you've got and not being too bedazzled by what you see in print.

If you think foliage is just a bunch of greens, it's not. In fact by concentrating only on flowers, your garden will have a monotonous look when they've faded even if you've done your best to plant things in succession.

(Zone 8) Pamela Frost shows how different glaucous or blue foliage plants work well together.
Left is the fern OSMUNDA REGALIS; *front centre* HOSTA HALCYON; *behind is* ASTRANTIA SHAGGY;
ground cover LYSIMACHIA NUMMULARIA AUREUM, *Creeping Jenny.*
In the rear, HOSTA UNDULATA *'Albomarginata'.*

You may have noticed by now that my favorite foliage is the greys and silvers. They have a leavening effect even next to neon-tinted phlox. The greys seem to refresh the garden when it's sagging in mid-August. Another of their great virtues is that the color becomes more intense with lack of water and summer heat. But too much of even a good thing will end up in ashes which is what an all-grey garden would give you.

GREY AND SILVER FOLIAGE ❧ Sun-lovers; sharp drainage is essential. SALIX LANATA, Arctic Willow, is a useful medium-sized 4-foot (1.2 meter) shrub; SANTOLINA CHAMAECYPARISSUS, Lavender Cotton—one of my all-time favorite plants—is a silvery little shrub that produces nothing much in the way of flowers. Even in the humblest garden it looks aristocratic and makes a great edging to a knot-garden; as a specimen; at the front of the border—in fact anywhere (see Listings Zone 6); HELICHRYSUM PETIOLATUM, Licorice Plant, is almost silver-white and a beautiful foil to the dusty tones of any variety of DIANTHUS. Alas, it isn't hardy so treat it as an annual. There are other HELICHRYSUM that are more muted and look wonderful with roses. SENECIO 'Sunshine' needs to be kept chopped back to look good. The same with S. CINERARIA, Dusty Miller. Then there are all the other favorites in the ARTEMISIA family. I'd have them all if I could find and accommodate them. ARTEMISIA LUDOVICIANA LATIFOLIA, Sagebrush, needs to be cut back severely in midsummer or it gets too sprawly. Clip A. 'Silver Mound' to keep its shape or it, too, will flop about in midseason. ANAPHALIS MARGARITACEA, Common Pearly Everlasting, sits well with the autumnal blues and purples of ASTER, Michaelmas Daisies. ROSA RUBRIFOLIA, Red Leaf Rose, has an almost thornless purple-red stem with mauve-grey leaves. In the shade it may be subdued but in full sun it will prove a marvellous foil for anything you plant around it—especially either Lavender or NEPETA, Catmint, as low plants, A. ABSINTHIUM behind. ONOPORDUM ACANTHIUM, Scotch Cotton-thistle, which grows to a humongous 8 feet (2.4 meters) in height, is a stunner of a biennial. It will self-seed. STACHYS LANATA, Lamb's-ears, is a great plant I like to alternate with lavender along a sidewalk in raised beds—gives the right romantic touch.

You may find grey and silver much too muted for your taste. There are glorious alternatives in the bronzes, purples, gold and variegations. They are all sun-lovers whose textures can vary from leathery to feathery.

PURPLE FOLIAGE ❧ You'll know with your

*Previous pages: (**Zone 6**) Dr. Henry Landis, Q.C.'s large suburban garden is filled with an astonishing variety of magnificent foliage: Mountain Ash;* CHAMAECYPARIS NOOTKATENSIS PENDULA, *Weeping Nootka False Cypress;* PINUS PARVIFLORA; *with ornamental spruces in front. To the right:* PINUS CONTORTA, *ornamental pines; blue spruce in background.*

*Opposite: (**Zone 8**) Contrasting and harmonious foliage plants in Kathie Leishman's garden create an arrestingly beautiful composition. From the top:* AZALEA GHENT; TAXUS JUNIPER; ACER PALMATUM, *Japanese Maple; left:* VIBURNUM DAVIDII; CORNUS ALBA SIBIRICA; PELTIPHYLLUM PELTATUM; *center:* IRIS PSEUDACORUS.

*(**Zone 6**) Carole Dancer chooses year-round colors for all her borders.*
This one has Heather Silver Queen; Golden Heather Robert Chapman; ERICA, *Springwood white; Yew;*
CHAMAECYPARIS *'Boulevard'; Junipers;* PRUNUS CISTENA, *sandstone cherry.*

botanical Latin that 'PURPUREUM' after any plant name will tell what the leaves look like. CHAENOMELES JAPONICA, Japanese Quince, needs to be cut back after its remarkable blooming in spring. This is a good shrub to espalier. BERBERIS THUNBERGII 'ATROPURPUREA', Red-Leaf Barberry, is another gorgeous hit of color. I also like COTINUS COGGYGRIA, Smokebush,

planted alongside an ELAEAGNUS ANGUSTIFOLIA, Russian Olive, with its silvery underfoliage. They make a splendid combination. Underplant with small bulbs in spring.

One of the most startling of annuals is RICINUS COMMUNIS, the Castor Bean plant. It's utterly poisonous but not, alas, to slugs. The huge serrated bronze leaves make a lively specimen like some exotic intruder. It's a good screening plant.

AJUGA REPTANS 'Atropurpurea', Carpet Bugle, spreads like mad in sun or semishade and more slowly in deep shade. It's a useful filler but needs to be carefully contained. I prefer either the pink or the variegated version. Other plants with brilliant and refreshing colors are: EUPHORBIA AMYGDALOIDES, Spurge ; SEDUM MAXIMUM 'Atropurpureum', Great Stonecrop; HEUCHERA MICRANTHA 'Palace Purple', Bronze Coral Bells; CORNUS ALBA 'Variegata' (sometimes called SIBIRICA 'Variegata'), Variegated Dogwood.

BRONZE FOLIAGE ❧ FOENICULUM VULGARE PURPUREUM, Bronze Fennel, has enough feathery foliage to soften the more fiery colors of autumn. RHEUM PALMATUM, Ornamental

(Zone 6) Tom Baskett's collection of RHODODENDRON, *broadleaf evergreens with* CONVALLARIA, *lily of the valley, and ferns planted beneath pine and birch. The grass path makes a pleasant contrast to the sensuous quality of the foliage.*

Rhubarb, has bronze red leaves in spring. Slugs, by the way, are also crazy about this plant so beware.

BLUE FOLIAGE ❧ Glaucous leaves harmonize with whites, mauves, pinks and violets. On the West Coast, EUCALYPTUS should be one of the favorites. It does as well as HEBE and the ACAENA with their more ferny foliage. HOSTA SIEBOLDIANA 'Elegans', Plantain Lily, is another wondrous blue-leaved plant which adds architectural qualities to its virtues. RUTA GRAVE-OLENS 'Jackman's Blue', Rue, is the most interesting of this species and needs sun.

THE SCARLETS ❧ I have a dwarf ACER PALMA-TUM, Japanese Maple, in my garden that is close to the perfect plant. As a specimen it makes its own quiet statement. It changes color all season ending with a magnificent burst of scarlet in fall and looks good even without leaves in winter.

VARIEGATION ❧ Many gardeners do not like variegated plants. In fact they eschew them altogether. Not me. I like ARABIS, Rock-cress, for instance, with its pretty white and pink spring flowers. The variegated ARABIS, a very slow grower, is far more mysterious and interesting. It's fun to search out variegated species in all the following: EUONYMUS ; HEDERA, Ivy; IRIS PAL-LIDA 'Variegata' has glorious foliage and when chopped up each spring can be distributed all over the garden. The flower is a lovely bonus.

There are many variegated hostas to choose from; LAMIUM, Deadnettle; and grasses such as MISCANTHUS SINENSIS 'Variegatus', Striped Eulalia Grass.

THE GOLDS ❧ Gold automatically brings sunshine into any part of the garden: MILIUM EFFUSUM 'Aureum', Bowles Golden Grass, does this for shady places; CAREX 'Bowles Golden', Bowles' Golden Sedge and ARUNDINARIA VIRIDISTRIATA, Bamboo, need sun. HOSTA SIEBOLDIANA 'Frances Williams' which has a yellow margin and near-white flowers is a favorite of mine. LIGUSTRUM X VICARYI, the Golden Privet is another tidy little shrub. Birds are crazy about SAMBUCUS NIGRA, Golden Elder, and if you have the space you shouldn't be without one.

Then there's the royalty of the foliage family, the rhododendrons: the flowers are splendid in their spring glory but it's the leathery foliage that's the real attraction for me. In a small city garden there is a hardy dwarf form I love called RHODODENDRON 'ramapo' with dainty bluish leaves. Azaleas and such handsome specimens as KALMIA LATIFOLIA, Mountain Laurel, should be considered along with the ERICACEAE, the Heather family, for their magnificent foliage. All you need is nicely acid soil and some winter protection.

(Zone 9) Susan Ryley uses large-leafed golden HOSTA *as a contrast to the golden* ORIGANUM *and Golden Elder, with the* H. ALBOMARGINATA *as foil.*
H. *Golden Prayers;* ORIGANUM VULGARE *'Aureum';*
H. CRISPULA; *Orange* OSTEOSPERMUM *(annual).*

(Zone 4) Jon Lowry's combination of foliage plants within the same family.
Left is an ARTEMISIA *along with a collection of* EUPHORBIA.

GREEN FOLIAGE ✿ Green has as much or more diversity in tones as any color in the spectrum. ALCHEMILLA VULGARIS, Lady's-mantle, has a soft velvety glow; RODGERSIA, Rodger's Flower, has an exquisite bronze-green leaf; BERGENIA CORDIFOLIA, Heartleaf Bergenia, has a rich shiny emerald surface. Keep exploring the possibilities of putting different tones of green together. The more subtle the undercurrents of your garden, the more pleasure you will get over the long seasons.

Grasses, of course, must be considered for their foliage. They are becoming newly fashionable even though they were among the first ground covers to evolve. Grasses are indispensable in covering up bulb stems turning brown in late spring. The right grass will add graceful arching forms to an otherwise straightforward vista; and they tend not to overgrow the spaces you allot them. Grasses add movement to a garden. And many grasses come into their own in the fall when other plants have faded or the garden is so brilliantly colored the eye needs

a rest. They also contribute an element of serenity.

Grasses to consider: PANICUM VIRGATUM, Switch Grass; FESTUCA OVINA GLAUCA, Sheep's Fescue; HELICTOTRICHON SEMPERVIRENS, Blue Evergreen Oat Grass.

FOLIAGE MAINTENANCE

Plant evergreens out of the prevailing winter winds. All those little needles can dry out swiftly and leave you with nothing but brown dripping off the bough. Buy antidessicants for your own little spritz bottles rather than in spray cans. You'll know if they aren't getting enough water when all the lower boughs turn sepia. Keep peering through your evergreens to see how they are doing. They may fool you for awhile by looking good from a distance.

Some deciduous shrubs are grafted onto parent stock to make them particularly hardy. The parent may try to reproduce itself by throwing up suckers all around. This saps the energy of the whole plant. Keep the suckers pulled out by going back to the original plant and yanking them off.

You should mulch shrubs, of course, but in late winter or early spring lift the previous year's mulch and scratch organic fertilizers into the surface. Then reapply the mulch. Again—don't do this when the ground is terribly wet.

Protection: You may want to plant beautiful shrubs that are not quite right for your microclimate. Apply some winter protection to extend their hardiness by most of a zone. The sight of a garden filled with mummified plants is a horror. I can't understand why no one's invented a beautiful protector that really works. Until this happens, do the following:

A. Add straw if you can find it at a nursery or local farm; evergreen boughs saved from every Christmas tree in the neighborhood. I follow the sound of fall buzz saws and collect as much of these leftovers as I can find.

B. Fashion a tepee of stakes (the long bamboo ones from the nursery) and stuff it with these boughs or cover the whole thing with burlap.

C. Make your own slatted wooden frames.

PRUNING SHRUBS

Shrubs must be pruned if they are not to overwhelm everything. I got a pair of great secateurs as a gift from my son one year. I went clip-happy. I couldn't go into the garden without snick-snicking away at every branch—living or dead. This is the hack-and-hope school of pruning. It may work for some people, even for some plants—did me a lot of good even if a few plants didn't survive.

Pruning is not only significant for a plant's health, it's fun to do when you've got the right equipment (See page 38).

How you prune is important. You don't just clunk something off because you don't like it. Find a point on the branch or stem near a node (swelling) and make a snip just above—not too close nor too far away. This gives the branch a new place from which to grow. You have to think about this a bit because you're also re-creating the shape of the plant. Always start with clean equipment. Make a clean sharp cut on an angle away from the direction in which you want the branch to grow.

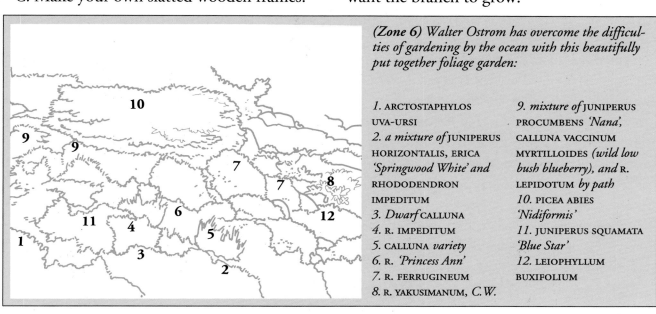

(Zone 6) Walter Ostrom has overcome the difficulties of gardening by the ocean with this beautifully put together foliage garden:

1. ARCTOSTAPHYLOS UVA-URSI
2. a mixture of JUNIPERUS HORIZONTALIS, ERICA *'Springwood White' and* RHODODENDRON IMPEDITUM
3. Dwarf CALLUNA
4. R. IMPEDITUM
5. CALLUNA *variety*
6. R. *'Princess Ann'*
7. R. FERRUGINEUM
8. R. YAKUSIMANUM, *C.W.*
9. mixture of JUNIPERUS PROCUMBENS *'Nana',* CALLUNA VACCINUM MYRTILLOIDES *(wild low bush blueberry), and* R. LEPIDOTUM *by path*
10. PICEA ABIES *'Nidiformis'*
11. JUNIPERUS SQUAMATA *'Blue Star'*
12. LEIOPHYLLUM BUXIFOLIUM

THE PRAIRIE GARDEN

The Prairies or The Great Plains lie west of the 90th meridian between the central lowlands and the western mountains. Action from the Ice Age scoured it clean. Failure to adapt meant extinction for plants as well as animals during this part of our history. Over the past ten thousand years the earth has attired itself with grasses that protect the precious soil. Humus is a priceless commodity on the Great Plains. The fine-textured clay soil when wet is fondly referred to as gumbo. It takes on moisture slowly, becomes soft when wet and erodes quickly on any degree of slope. When compacted it dries to bricklike solidity.

On what seems unpromising land, a surprising number of flowers have adapted. Low rainfall, lots of sunshine and severe winter temperatures require plant hardiness. Trees generally follow river courses. North of Edmonton and along the Saskatchewan River, however, the northern forest marks its boundary all across Saskatchewan to the Manitoba border. The Cypress Hills of Alberta, a 100 mile (161 kilometer) long strip rises to 4800 feet (1463 meters) at about 16 feet (5 meters) over 1 mile (1.6 kilometers). The terrain has a surface of small boulders and pebbles deposited during the glacial period. This allows for uninterrupted run-off during rains. Wind is the serious factor here pushing incredible volumes of soil around. Any land left uncovered is going to be lost. There are sandhills in Nebraska, badlands in Alberta and North Dakota but each has its own special desert-type plants.

Plants that adapted most readily were ones that liked Arctic conditions: lichens, ice mosses, sedges, willows and alders. During the ice retreat other plants appeared in succession: deciduous trees such as birch, maple, beech and finally oak.

For every type of soil there are several species of grass that can not only withstand drought but also the prairie fires that level shrubs and trees. Grasses and flowering plants of the Great Plains have acquired an essential faculty—the ability to withstand drought. Trees need either human intervention or a river course to stand up to prairie conditions. Long summer days of bright sunlight without the leavening influence of hills or trees to shade plants mean that temperatures can reach 100°F (37°C) during July and August. But cool nights provide time for the plants to regain their moisture balance.

Genera that thrive in this climate: phlox, aster, cactus, evening primrose, the pea family. All have many species in them. The most sensible Prairie Garden is one that echoes the natural surroundings. Combine plants that won't be blown over by winds—mat-forming buns that grow from a taproot. Look for plants with light-reflecting, waxy, blue-grey-green leaves and all the shades of pale grey through sparkling silver to white foliage. They have protective hairs; textures range from velvety to very coarse. Hairy plants do exceptionally well since this survival strategy shields them from intense light and evaporation.

Claude Barr, the distinguished plantsman of the Great Plains, had the following in his garden:

(Zone 4) Phyllis and Fred Enns commissioned landscape architect Jon Lowry to create this garden. The distant mountains appear to be at the end of the garden in the stone and gravel stream. From center top to right: PINUS MUGO PROSTRATA; P. MUGO MUGHOS; PICEA GLAUCA; YUCCA GLAUCA; ARTEMISIA CANA; SEDUM KAMTSCHATICUM; ARCTOSTAPHYLOS UVA-URSI.

'Harrison's Yellow' Rose, French lilac, annuals such as larkspurs, VERBENA, poppies and nasturtiums, as well as many of the native plants you'll find in the listings below.

Other plants to consider for a Prairie Garden: ACTAEA, Baneberry; ANISE HYSSOP, a herb with pleasant blue flowers that attracts bees; ARNICA, a rich orange-yellow daisy; ARTEMISIA FRIGIDA, Fringed Sagebrush; A. LONGIFOLIA and A. TRIDENTATA, Sagebrush, the big sagebrush of the West. ASCLEPIAS PUMILA, Milkweed, has masses of honey-scented blooms. Asters include ASTER FENDLERI; ASTRALAGUS, Milk Vetch, an important *genera;* ATRIPLEX, Saltbush, an olive-grey shrub with enough salt content to attract rabbits so be prepared. BAPTISIA, False Indigo, has adapted to the plains, and of course OPUNTIA, Prickly Pear Cactus, has pores that close to retain moisture. O. FRAGILIS, Brittle Prickly-pear, is all over the northern plains states east to Manitoba. CASTILLEJA, Indian Paintbrush; ECHINACEA ANGUSTIFOLIA, Purple Coneflower, is a wonderful plant. GALIUM, Lady's Bedstraw, good substitute for GYPSOPHILA or Baby's-breath, tends to be weedy and needs to be cut back to keep it from going brown underneath. POTENTILLA FRUTICOSA, Bush Cinquefoil, has a limy preference in soils and is practically drought-proof. PULSATILLA PATENS, Pasque Flower, is the emblem of both Saskatchewan and South Dakota, for good reason—it flourishes on the prairies.

In these areas, fresh seeds germinate readily but seedlings are difficult to transplant. Don't disturb their roots and take lots of soil if you must move them. The famous wild rose, the emblem of Alberta and North Dakota is an obvious choice for a prairie garden. SENECIO GRANSEL, Ragwort; SMILACINA STELLATA, False Solomon's Seal, is another example of drought-tolerant adaptation. SOLIDAGO MOLLIS, Dwarf Goldenrod, is a very beautiful low form of this common native plant.

CLIMATE FACTS TO FACE

Sandy soil takes up moisture readily but doesn't retain it; limestone chips help hold it and at the same time supply lime to the soil. Peat moss is an excellent moisture retainer but don't apply it dry. Soak it for about a week and start off with boiling water.

Drainage is essential for dry country plants and raised beds could solve this problem. Other remedies: re-dig your beds and put down a substratum of gravel or tile. Thin tiles of stone buried at an angle also help drainage. Or put 6 inches (15 centimeters) of sand on top of regular garden soil.

Create a scree: Remove eight inches (20 centimeters) of soil then add loam or compost with scree mix. Trample it down to ground level. Scree mix: two parts sand, one part each of limestone chips, milled peat moss, and good clay loam.

Midday heat is always a problem on the Prairies: a slope away from the sun is helpful, the shade of some distant object, or a lath house if it's simply too hot. This is a structure that could take the shape of a pergola with a top and sides consisting of lathes at about 2-inch (5-centimeter) intervals.

(Zone 3) Nadine Crawford designed this Japanese garden with the pretty lily pond. From the top: grass, Ribbon Grass, HEMEROCALLIS, Daylily; IRIS, German Bearded Iris; DIANTHUS, Pink; SEDUM KAMTSCHATICUM, clipped ball juniper in the oriental style; FESTUCA GLAUCA OVINA.

THE WINTER GARDEN

In designing a garden, think of winter first of all. There are too many months when we can only look at our gardens and not get out there and muck about in them. In choosing your plants think about ones with beautiful form. Imagine them stripped of foliage and if you like the shape then that's what to get for winter interest. They should look dramatic on their own. A miserable winter day can be considerably improved by the sight of brightly colored berries, evergreen foliage, colored stems on shrubs and trees, even dead flowerheads and grasses. These are all a significant part of the winter landscape.

Weeping plants with their long trailing branches can improve the dreariest landscape. BETULA PENDULA 'GRACILIS', Weeping Birch (Zones 2-9); PICEA PENDULA, Weeping Spruce (Zones 2-9); CHAMAECYPARIS NOOTKATENSIS

(Zone 6) Walter Ostrom has built the ideal lath house.
CLEMATIS *'Comtesse de Bouchard';* Shasta Daisy; POTENTILLA, *Spirea;* C. *'JACKMANII';*
C. TANGUTICA *clambering all over it; below: a daisylike annual that grows wild in Ireland.*

'PENDULA', Weeping Nootka False Cypress (Zones 5-9) are all fascinating in winter. CORYLUS AVELLENA 'CONTORTA' standard, Corkscrew Hazel (Zones 5-9) in a top grafted standard form is a pleasure on a sunny winter day. Broadleaf evergreens such as rhododendrons with their leathery textured leaves come in many colors and in warmer zones don't have to be wrapped in hideous burlap blankets.

Train HEDERA HELIX, English Ivy, up a wall or around a deciduous tree; COTONEASTER HORIZONTALIS, Rockspray Cotoneaster, set against a fence, trained in a wide spray looks gorgeous; vines such as CELASTRUS SCANDENS, Bittersweet, have crimson berries all winter long. Remember ornamental grasses that stay evergreen or which you leave in dried form:

MISCANTHUS SINENSIS, Eulalia Grass looks good (Zone 4) all winter and lends itself to partnership with evergreens; PENNISETUM ALOPECUROIDES, Fountain Grass (Zones 5-6) is dependable from July until February; SPARTINA PECTINATA AUREO-MARGINATA, Prairie Cord Grass (Zone 4) is lovely but may succumb to a load of heavy snow; CAREX MORROWII VARIEGATA, Japanese Sedge (Zone 4) is shade-tolerant, weedproof and evergreen; FESTUCA OVINA GLAUCA, Blue Fescue (Zone 4) adds color to the winter garden.

To prepare your winter garden for winter, don't clean up your borders too carefully. Forests survive quite nicely without the aid of either broom or rake. Make sure, however, that you don't leave piles of junk around for slugs and other meddlers to nest in all winter. Moderate cleaning up seems to work most effectively.

*(**Zone 6**) Janet Rosenberg has sculpted shapes out of snow with a BUXUS, Boxwood hedge. The garden of Janice and Hugh Rennie has a PICEA GLAUCA, White Spruce in the foreground with HIBISCUS SYRIACUS, Rose of Sharon. A cedar hedge, PINUS NIGRA, Austrian pine, and PICEA PUNGENS, Colorado Spruce, form a dense background for the lightness of the plants beneath them, AMELANCHIER CANADENSIS, Serviceberry.*

(Zone 6) *This picture shows how the brilliant berries on*
ILEX, *Holly can show up in the winter landscape.*
In the foreground is Golden threadleaf CHAMAECYPARIS, *and*
behind dwarf blue juniper and RHODODENDRON.

Left: *(Zone 6)* *Barbara Frum's garden changes constantly*
and this is one of her great joys. When this shot was taken
there was a Dwarf Spruce on the left, now gone;
and on the right of the step a silver edged DAPHNE.
The area is dotted with MUGHO *pines and tree peonies.*
Behind is a LARIX, *weeping larch hybrid.*

SPECIAL GARDENS — SUGGESTIONS AND SOLUTIONS

*H*ow to make the best use of the space you have is limited mainly by very specific problems. We'll try to address a few of them here. This is not intended to solve all your dilemmas or all the difficulties of an oddly sited lot, but to cover a few of the major ones that were mentioned by gardeners.

Squint your eye when you look at your space. You will be seeing it in much the way a camera does. Not accurately but something will jump out at you. And that something might be what you should concentrate on.

When you are creating a garden from scratch, think about how you're going to water and light it. Installing a good drip system is so much easier to do before you add the other major elements. The same applies to lighting. Burying and marking electric cords is a lot easier before you add plants especially large ones.

Think of your garden in layers. There is the canopy, the understorey and the floor: trees (canopy), the larger shrubs (understorey), large perennials, dwarf or sub-shrubs (more understoreys); and ground covers (the floor)—behave just like a forest. Each occupies a level of space and opens up the number of plants you can use.

It gives your garden texture and density.

Never level a plot of land. If you're buying so-called empty land, don't let your contractor or the developer pull everything out. You see sad real estate ads trumpeting "level lot." Just what you don't want. Working with what nature's left behind is important. At least you've got the backbone of your space intact and will probably have some fairly mature shrubs and trees. Clearing carefully, keeping any attractive native plants will mean you don't have to wait for years to get suitable results.

Each site has its own interesting problems and you can have a lot of fun during the winter giving your fantasy life full rein. Here are suggestions for solving just a few of the problems you may encounter.

THE SHADE GARDEN

No matter what zone you live in there will be shade in your garden. This is a terrific bonus. A shady bower is perhaps one of the most refreshing places to be during the height of summer heat. It might be part of a courtyard, a north-facing border, beneath a pergola or under a canopy of an ancient tree.

(Zone 9) Elizabeth England's side border with yellow foliage.
Center: CLEMATIS REHDERANA, *growing up a purple-leaved 'Royal Standard' Crab Apple tree;*
From left to right: HOSTA FILIPENDULA ULMARIA AUREO; HOSTA; SILENE *'Sissinghurst'; golden elder;*
POLYGONATUM, *Solomon's Seal, under the tree.*

*(**Zone 9**) George Radford's elegant shade garden.*
From the bottom of the photograph: HOSTA SIEBOLDIANA *'*ELEGANS*' behind* DICENTRA *(red);*
POLYGONATUM, *Solomon's Seal;* GERANIUM SANGINEUM, *Bloody Cranesbill;*
to the rear, DICENTRA, *white Bleeding Heart; self-seeding annual Stock,* CORYDALIS LUTEA.

This fits in with the concept that you plant like-minded plants near each other. Siting one that needs dry sun with one that likes moist semi-shade doesn't make a lot of sense. But sometimes you don't think of this when you're putting together lovely colors or foliage.

Another thing you need to know about your soil is its alkalinity content. A lot of the shade-lovers prefer acid or slightly acid soil. There are a number of things you can do but the most permanent treatment is to dig up the area and treat the soil from below by adding Epsom salts along with milled peat moss and manure to the soil. (See page 71 for more on how to create a more acid soil.)

And you're going to have to work over the soil pretty severely if it's under trees. Maples, for instance, not only suck up all the water they can but also sap the nutrients as well. Add extra compost, extra manure, and don't clean up the leaf litter too tidily.

What kind of shade do you have? There will be a difference in the kind of shade that a deciduous tree casts from that of a coniferous.

The latter is likely to be more dense.

Dense shade: Excludes almost all except reflected light.

Medium shade: North-facing locations perhaps with an overhang of branches or a high fence.

Open shade: Fairly bright north-facing location with no direct sun.

Dappled: Bright but without any direct sun, certainly not for any length of time. A great many sun-loving plants do very well in this light and would be indicated by sun-shade.

The kind of shade you have will change with each season. In winter a north-facing border in my garden gets no sun at all, it keeps its snow cover the longest, and stays very moist. And it's also first to get hit with light frost. In summer, sunlight arrives late in the afternoon.

You can control the shade to some extent by careful pruning of large trees. Thinning out branches can make a remarkable difference in the amount of light that seeps into your shade garden. For instance, a birch tree affords the most enchanting filtered shade and all sorts of things will grow around it. Right under a huge

maple, however, early spring bulbs do just fine but other plants struggle once it comes into full leaf. The maple and the weeping willow in my garden keep out a lot of rain. If they weren't sitting in a fairly wet situation anyway I'd be much more careful about watering on a regular basis than I am now.

Dry shade: If you've got tree roots too close to the surface for the comfort of your plants try using raised beds of peat moss and leaf mould, along with good soil and compost. If the soil is too poor, you may have to dig it out and replace it with good soil and plenty of humus. HAMAMELIS MOLLIS, Witchhazel; POLYGONATUM, Solomon's Seal; GERANIUM MACRORRHIZAN, Bigroot Geranium, survive poor soil; as does G. ENDRESSII, Cranesbill; EUPHORBIA CHARACIAS, v. Wulfenii; and the enchanting COLCHICUM, the Autumn Crocus.

When you buy plants, pick ones already growing in the shade or in a lath house. If you don't have any shade in your garden, a lath house, or a pergola can substitute until your trees mature and give protection from the sun.

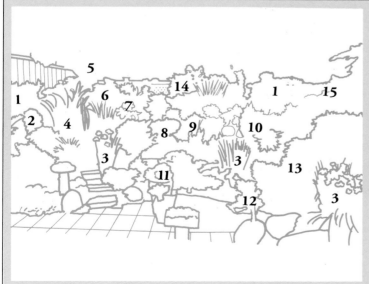

(Zone 8) Don Armstrong created this serene garden (see previous pages) when he removed the backyard swimming pool:

1. RHODODENDRON
2. ACTINIDIA KOLOMITKA
3. IRIS *hybrid*
4. I. PSEUDACORUS
5. MAGNOLIA GRANDIFLORA
6. SMILICINA *False Solomon's-seal*
7. RODGERSIA
8. HEBE
9. ADIANTUM PEDATUM, *Maidenhair fern*
10. DRYOPTERIS FELI
11. ABIES LASIOCARPA
12. GENISTA FILOSA *'Vancouver Gold', Broom*
13. NANDINA DOMESTICA, *Heavenly Bamboo*
14. PAEONIA LUTEA, *tree Peony*
15. AUCUBA JAPONICA

(Zone 8) In this shady corner of his garden, Don Armstrong shows how diverse shade plants
can be in both foliage and color. Next to the antique lion is a fern, DRYOPTERIS WALLICHIANA.
From left to right front: CORYDALIS, BERGENIA, *with a collection of hostas;*
the ground cover is ADIANTUM VENUSTUM; VANCOUVERIA TRACII. *Next to the* RHODODENDRON
EPIMENDIUM *is an* ARISAEMA.

Remember that the sun has a different degree of intensity in the morning—the afternoon is much hotter. If the sun happens to hit your shade-loving plants they might wilt or get sunburned. Water and shield them immediately.

Give shade plants lots of room when you put them in the ground. They require more space than sun-lovers to get all the nutrients they need. They must have good air circulation or you'll be plagued with mildew.

Ground covers do well if you've got a lot of trees. For years, I've watched neighbors who put in grass seed and sod under huge conifers and who can't understand why it won't grow. Just look in any forest. Grass doesn't grow in deep shade. Start with ground covers that spread quickly and will eliminate weeds:

LYSIMACHIA NUMMULARIA, Creeping Jenny, has pretty yellow flowers in spring but you'll probably end up having to pull it out by the bucket. In the meantime it will do a good job of covering bare soil. GALAX, an evergreen ground cover, is quite wonderful with its shiny round leaves with serrated edges that will crawl almost anywhere. BERGENIA, Heartleaf bergenia, an expensive but dramatic plant; PACHYSANDRA

TERMINALIS, Japanese Spurge, will grow just about anywhere—I'm not crazy about it but if it's grown thickly it can look very clean; MYSOTOSIS, Forget-me-nots, are pretty and they cover up bulb stems nicely, but they eventually get straggly; BRUNNERA or Siberian Bugloss is even better and has the same effective little blue flowers. EPIMEDIUM, Barrenwort, is a lovely plant that spreads slowly but it won't take dry shade; VINCA MINOR, Periwinkle—shiny leaves, pleasant blue flowers—takes a long time to actually get going, but be patient since it is worthwhile; v. 'BOWLES' variety combined with Bowles' Golden Grass will bring a little sunshine into any gloomy spot. ARCTOSTAPHYLOS UVA-URSI, Kinikinick, likes an acid soil and has rich green foliage. The hardiest of all ground covers.

Hostas are a favorite of mine and there are dozens in the genera. There are many plants that act as ground covers so don't reject anything with strong spreading power. Dwarf ASTILBE make a splendid shady ground cover. The little plumes of colors from white to a deep

(Zone 9) George Radford likes to combine interesting textures in his plant combinations. EUPHORBIA CHARACIAS *seems to come out of a clump of* CAMPANULA PORTENSCHLAGIANA; HOSTA SEIBOLDIANA 'ELEGANS'; *pot* SALIX LANATA; CORYDALIS; *the perpetual rose is an eglantine Stanwell;* DICENTRA; *pot* PINUS CONTORTA *in front of the fence.*

red will provide a luminous area when they blossom; and a subtle ground cover if you cut the blooms off.

Trees: BETULA PENDULA, Weeping Birch; AMELANCHIER CANADENSIS, Serviceberry; SORBUS, Mountain Ash; QUERCUS, Oaks are ideal since they are deep-rooted and grow slowly. Deciduous trees mean lots of material for leaf mould. ROBINIA, Locust; CERCIS CANADENSIS, Redbud Judas tree, are two very good specimens.

Shrubs: AMELANCHIER, Saskatoonberry; CEONOTHUS AMERICANUS 'GLOIRE DE VERSAILLES', Wild Lilac, likes a sandy soil and semi-shade—it has gorgeous blue flowers and if you're in any part of the country that will grow this plant do so. CHAENOMELES JAPONICA, Japanese Quince, makes a great show in the spring and it's also the best plant for espaliering along a shady wall. PYRACANTHA, Firethorn, has berries that attract birds as does SAMBUCUS, Elder. There are superb evergreen rhododendrons that do well in acid soil in shade: RHODODENDRONS CATAWBIENSE; R. YAKUSIMANUM; some of the azaleas. KALMIA LATIFOLIA, Mountain Laurel, also likes acid soil. Include ERICA, Heather, for very light shade and ANDROMEDA POLIFOLIA, Bog Rosemary.

One of my favorites is HYDRANGEA PETIOLARIS, Climbing Hydrangea—a vine that will serve you well in shade ramping up a tree; CELASTRUS SCANDENS, Bittersweet, provides winter interest with its bright red berries. And of course you'll want HEDERA HELIX, English Ivy, for a lush green carpet in dark corners.

There are plenty of perennials useful for underplanting. I'll mention a few here. Check the Listings in each zone:

ANGELICA ARCHANGELICA, Wild Parsnip, is a biennial that self-seeds. It's rather coarse but dramatic. CYPRIPEDIUM, Lady's Slipper, is an absolute must in the shade garden but be sure and mark it since it disappears in summer during dormancy. DIGITALIS, Foxglove, is another useful biennial—plant this year for blooms next year; let it self-seed and you have a sense of continuous growth. DODECATHEON, Shooting Star, will brighten a dark corner. GENTIANA ASCLEPIADEA, the Willow Gentian, has clear blue flowers with cheerful demeanor.

Some ornamental grasses that do very well in shade: CAREX PENDULA, Sedge, protect from wind and winter sun; C. MORROWII VARIEGATA, Japanese Sedge; C. MUSKINGUMENSIS, Palm Sedge, is a native good most of the year; MISCANTHUS SINENSIS VARIEGATA, Eulalia Grass.

WATER IN THE GARDEN

Using water creatively has become one of the choicest uses of space in the contemporary garden. Fountains, ponds, even a tiny reflecting pool add an element of serenity to the urban garden. Having a small fountain plunking away can mask out a great many of the irritating noises that pollute the atmosphere.

(Zone 5) Looking down the water coursing through Amy Stewart's garden.
On the left: PULMONARIA *and* BERGENIA, CORYDALIS LUTEA; BERGENIA;
to the right ALCHEMILLA MOLLIS; *variegated Dogwood, a grass and a hosta.*
Siberian Iris, LIGULARIA *with* FILIPENDULA *in the background.*

Previous pages: (Zone 8) Barbara Durrant's pool is a sanctuary for many levels of fascinating plants.
From left: ARMERIA; RHODODENDRON; SAXIFRAGA
London Pride; CAMPANULA PRIMULIFOLIA; IRIS *and a rare white* MECANOPSIS.

It can be accomplished relatively easily with something as humble as a buried garbage can with a pump attachment and pipes to keep the water flowing over rocks. To make another simple pool dig the proper size hole, add gravel for drainage in case of leaks, line it with heavy-duty plastic and set rocks around the edges to conceal the plastic. An inexpensive black fiberglass sink with drain and a circulating pump can be the receptacle for water splashing over a piece of sculpture.

Add some water plants set in pots. They usually need a lot of sun but there are many moisture-loving plants that will tolerate a shady spot and will work beautifully along the edges for a splendid effect.

The pump will keep the water aerated, but it isn't absolutely necessary as long as you add some water each day.

GARDEN ON THE ROCKS

There are natural rock outcroppings all over North America. But the ones left behind by the ancient ice sheets are a particularly dramatic context for the garden. If you live in one of the

(Zone 6) Walter Ostrom's rock wall is built at the perfect height to appreciate precious and very small rock plants. Foreground: JUNIPERUS PROCUMBENS *'Nana'; on the wall:* CAMPANULA COCHLEARIIFOLIA; DASYANTHA; ABIES BALSAMEA *'Nana';* PICEA ABIES *'Little Gem';* DIANTHUS; EMPETRUM EAMESII.

*(Zone 9) Ernie Lithgoe has built a rock garden to perfect scale.
He put in as many* CAMPANULA *as he could along with* CORYDALIS *in the foreground with a
mat of* THYMUS LANUGINOSUS, *woolly Thyme;* PHLOX SUBULATA TOMENTOSA;
conifer dwarf Yew; CORYDALIS OCHROLEUCA; *the intense violet plant is* MOLTKIA PETRAEA;
CAMPANULA BETULIFOLIA; *seed head is* ANTHYLLIS MONTANA.

many areas of the country where gigantic rocks push their way into your garden don't despair. This is a magnificent detail. Creating a peat garden is one solution—find hollows and fill them with peat and plant peat-loving plants such as ARCTOSTAPHYLOS UVA-URSI, Kinikinick or VACCINIUM ANGUSTIFOLIUM, Lowbush Blueberry.

Choose plants that have a central root and like to spread such as PHLOX SUBULATA, Creeping Phlox. It will spill down a rock face in the most satisfactory way. For other plants add soil and peat to make up a mixture that will sustain a larger variety of plants. Minerals from the rock face itself will nourish the plants.

(**Zone 9**) *Penstemons are ideal for the rock garden or in the front of the border. There are over 250 species and it's a plant many get hooked on—understandably.*

To the left: (**Zone 9**) *Jack Todd literally gardens on the rock:* PICEA *dwarf blue spruce,* CHAMAECYPARIS PISIFERA 'FILIFERA'; POTENTILLA *backed by lavender;* ARUNCUS DIOICUS; SEDUM *'Autumn Joy';* ARABIS; GERANIUM; DIANTHUS; CAMPANULA *as well as a splendid collection of alpine plants.* CHAMAECYPARIS HINOKI, *Cypress behind the white plant.*

MAKING A ROCK GARDEN ❧ Rock walls, slopes with well-placed rocks are all part of the potential for a rock garden. Anybody interested in rock gardening should really look at these plants in the wild. They grow in almost pure rock chips with water moving through the soil. Sharp drainage is the most important thing to be aware of. To make a mixture for your rock garden soil use at least one third coarse grit bigger than pea gravel. If you can find some, fractured rock is the best.

A superb solution to displaying rock plants, which tend to be small and exquisite, is to plant them on top of a rock wall. It keeps them from getting lost in the larger areas of the garden—they become special treasures. Use them in trough gardens built with Tufa, a composition stone made of limestone which also feeds the alpines with necessary minerals.

You don't need a big space for a rock garden. Two hundred plants will fit into a 65 foot (20 meter) rock garden 6 feet (1.8 meters) wide.

(Zone 3) This is a restoration of a Japanese garden installed during the 1930s conforming to the shape of the ravine it runs up. Water slowly threads its way through the garden to this muted planting of junipers, pine, tamarisk, larch; daylilies and AEGOPODIUM PODOGRARIA, *variegated Goutweed.*

(Zone 6) In Mr. and Mrs. Gordon Campbell's garden the lettuce is strictly for decoration.
From right to left: LAVANDULA MUNSTEAD; *Rambler Rose;* CAMPANULA; *delphinium;*
poppy; petunia; AQUILEGIA; GYPSOPHILA.

Rock garden plants are indicated in the Listings for each zone.

RAVINE GARDEN

If you have a garden that runs up or down a hill, think seriously about putting in terraces or steps along the slope. A stone or brick pathway can lead to different sections: to a hosta bed in a shady area underplanted with the first spring bulbs for instance. Have a place to get to as a *raison d'être* for the pathway—a small bower, pergola, a gazebo, a bench.

Keep in mind that you'll probably have good drainage; think of a simple Japanese design with a small fall of water.

SMALL CITY GARDEN

Probably more has been written on this subject than any other in gardening history. It's a fascinating site. Don't put everything you love in here, it will look fussy. Too much will make the eye dance over the landscape rather than resting on a single artifact or planting. Something simple will create a serene place which is what you want in a crowded city.

*(**Zone 3**)* GYPSOPHILA *is the ideal foil for almost any other plant in the summer border. They don't like to be disturbed so it's wise to know exactly where you want them before you plant.*

*Right: (**Zone 6**) Aileen Harris's patio garden is tiny but every inch of space is utilized. Left to right: Geraniums in pot; lavender;* ARTEMISIA *Silver King;* VERONICA SPICATA; *Silver lace vine up the hydro pole; yew; tree roses with hydrangea, spirea, hosta; Thyme in a pot; more variegated hostas; salmon pink* PENSTEMON; CLEMATIS JACKMANII; C. TANGUTICA.

*Below: (**Zone 6**) J. Schofield Manuel's garden
designed by Murray Haig is a stunning
combination of annuals among clipped Korean
Boxwood;* ECHEVERIA; *pink and white*
BEGONIA; *with annual variegated grass in the
center. Vine on the house is* EUONYMUS
FORTUNEI *'Emerald Gaiety'.*

Left: At the rear of the house over the pool
SYRINGA LUTINA *standards with clipped box;*
IMPATIENS; ARTEMISIA *'Silver Mound';*
DIANTHUS, *Pink; white hybrid begonias,
sunshine impatiens and silver edged hostas*
(ALBOMARGINATA); *Cotoneaster falls over the
stairs; the south facing walls of the garden are
planted with Boston Ivy and* EUONYMUS
'SARCOXIE'; *north facing walls are planted
with climbing* HYDRANGEA PETIOLARIS *and
English Ivy.* RHODODENDRON CATAWBIENSE
ALBA; *the globe Cedar is* WOODWARDII *next to
the base of the sculpture.*
Also white BLANC DOUBLE DE COUBERT
Roses; white phlox; dwarf spirea.

In a small city garden you will probably be more aware of what's happening at your neighbor's place. Mask out anything ugly or intrusive such as a garage, windows or dull walls by adding some height to your fence with trellis work and putting up vines that will come into bloom in succession. Or painting in a witty *faux* ruin such as the one illustrated below.

Raised beds can add a sculptural dimension to a very small garden. It will probably be unnecessary to have grass but you will want interesting paving stones, bricks or other terracing material as a contrast to plants. I like ground covers in just about every shape and color. Consider collecting the huge family of thymes especially the following: THYMUS CITRONUS, T. MONTANA ALBA and T. M. ROSA; AJUGA, Bugleweed, is another excellent ground cover and it comes in a particularly pretty variegated version as well as A. REPTANS, 'Burgundy Glow'. But you can have too much of this one. Even in a tiny garden a small pond or

*Above: (**Zone 6**) Murray Haig's handpainted folly adds a sense of humor to a very romantic garden.*
His faux *ruin separates a parking space covered by a parachute which doubles as a dance floor.*
In front of the gates SEDUM VARIEGATUM *'Autumn Joy';* SEDUM SPECTABILE VARIEGATUM; *bittersweet*
CELASTRUS SCANDENS; *an unnamed* SEDUM *from a friend's garden seems quite happy in the gravel.*

*Previous page: (**Zone 6**) A garage transformed into a pavilion expands the use of*
Joanne Shaw's small garden designed by Murray Haig. RHODODENDRON CATAWBIENSE;
single Rose of Sharon; Bergenia; hostas mainly SEIBOLDIANA ELEGANS; PACHYSANDRA TERMINALIS;
EUONYMUS 'SARCOXIE'; BERGENIA CORDIFOLIA; *wisteria and* RHODODENDRON PJM; *roses,*
BLANC DOUBLE DE COUBERT; COTONEASTER DAMMERI.

fountain in scale with the rest of the space will give an aura of tranquility. You might consider a foliage garden with exotic grasses and small shrubs rather than borders filled with perennials that may overwhelm your space. Mirrors, as you can see in this skillfully designed garden, will make any border appear twice as wide; so will a reflecting pool.

Nurturing standards—mature plants grown on one stem—or topiary (not in the shape of ducks or swans) in a small garden is a splendid long-range project. They will also allow you to add many more levels to your planting. Espaliering of course works particularly well in a very small garden. You can tuck ornaments around in a beguiling way drawing the viewer into the garden.

*(**Zone 6**) Jill Robinson created this tapestry in green in an area that was once a parking lot:*
From left to right: MAGNOLIA ACUMINATII; CHAMAECYPARIS PISIFERA 'PLUMOSA'; RHODODENDRON
FORTUNEI; C. PISIFERA 'AUREA'; R., *Janet Blair;* R. IMPEDITUM; R. IMPEDITUM X MOUPINENSE;
IRIS KAEMPFERI; R. SCHLIPPENBACHII; R. ROSEUM; R. FRASERI; C. OBTUSA 'COMPACTA'; R. ATLANTICUM;
R. LUTEUM; R. DAURICUM; CORNUS KOUSA, *Chinese Dogwood.*

*(**Zone 6**) Neil Turnbull designed this dazzling foliage border with the architecture of each plant complementing the one next to it.*

Arches open up a vista even if it's only for a short distance. The eye will add an extra dimension if there are climbing vines behind them.

Another way to enhance this illusion of distance is to have a reflecting pool narrower at the distant end. The optical illusion will be one of length. It will create a fascinating tension with the surrounding plants.

Huge pots of herbs add a dramatic element in an informal garden; and a knot garden in scale with the space would not only be a charming summer garden but would also be a definite plus in winter.

LARGE SQUARE GARDEN

If you build a swimming pool consider adding some dyes into the concrete before it's poured. A black pool fits into the landscape much more easily than a blazing turquoise. It also acts as a reflector for any choice shrubs and trees you may have put in nearby.

If you want a softer look, add a terra cotta color to the tiles that edge the pool. Perhaps have your pool designed in other than a rigid rectangle, some gentler shape that will fit into the natural landscape.

A pergola can act as a transition space to the

rest of the garden; a free-standing trellis can divide the garden into convenient sections for subtle changes in interest such as a vegetable garden.

Make your borders as large as you possibly can; have walks of grass between them or free standing borders along fences with different shapes. In her garden Jill Robinson had to contend with a parking lot on one side, and a huge condo that blocked a former view of the sea at the rear. A large circular border in the middle distracts the eye and creates a peaceful retreat.

LONG NARROW LOT

Here's what I did with mine: I divided it into three spaces—the hot section with paving stones confining plants that like to ramp. A woodland section with berm—very cool and quiet with peaceful muted colors. I'm lucky because I have enough room here for an open potting shed. A fence divides this section from raised beds at the rear. I have a cutting garden, nursery bed (where seedlings are set out in spring, and where I like to experiment with new plants to see how they'll do) and small vegetable garden. The compost is confined to three spots—one area for piling leaves; a small container and a spot to store leftover compost.

PIE-SHAPED LOT

This is a perfect space in which to create a logical vista. At the point of the pie have something to pull your eye towards: a fountain, a bower of roses, a classic birdbath; a wonderful specimen tree or shrub, something really dramatic and special; or of course the most romantic thing of all—a gazebo with a climbing vine ramping away over it. A central circular bed could echo the round beds at the sides of the lot.

On a lot with the house at the apex, create a screen with well-placed contrasting foliage shrubs and trees.

A COUNTRY GARDEN

Fitting into the landscape is crucial in a country garden. Putting up something utterly different from the surrounding landscape, exotic you might say, won't do justice to your site. Materials on patios and decks should be totally sympathetic with the architecture of the house. You can use local materials—rocks, wood, stones—anything that will harmonize with the style of the house.

Capitalize on any undulations of the land around you. In fact you may have all the elements mentioned above—rock facing, slopes, flat areas, woods and exposed sites.

Have the space between your formal garden and the countryside turned into a meadow. You'll probably have enough space for a serious lawn, enormous sweeping borders, as well as a more intimate garden close to the house. A body of water is a must in the country since it will be easy to dig out and furnish with water-loving plants around its edges such as LYSIMACHIA PUNCTATA, Yellow Loosestrife; IRIS PSEUDACORUS, Water Iris, I. SIBIRICA, Siberian Iris; RODGERSIA, Rodger's-flower and GUNNERA, which make their own dramatic statement.

(Zone 6) Arthur Dauphinee's garden. The garden furniture is from an earlier more gracious period. In the background is LYTHRUM, *and the two climbers are* LONICERA, *Honeysuckle, and a rambler rose.*

HARDINESS ZONES

We all live in a general hardiness zone. These hardiness zones are a convenient way of indicating what kinds of plants can survive under certain kinds of conditions of light and temperature. It is also a very, very loose designation of areas that share similar elements of climate: the number of frost-free days a year and annual low and high winter temperatures.

There are serious factors, however, that the climate zones don't consider and you'll have to figure them out for yourself through careful observation. For instance the following are all important to the health and longevity of your plants:

SLOPES ❧ If you live on a hillside you'll find that you have longer frost-free periods, but the valley below will be colder at night and warmer during the day, more so than at midslope or on hilltops. Cold air pours down a slope and gathers in pools at the bottom. This is called a frost hollow. At the top there will be cooler maximum temperatures and a shorter frost-free period than at midslope. At midslope more snow will accumulate affording greater plant protection. If you are in a mountainous region, one side will be dry, the other wetter. Winds suck moisture out of the air as they rise and dump that moisture as they fall.

ASPECT ❧ This is the direction you face in relation to the sun. A south facing slope will mean warmer air but in winter it may also mean denser snow and more of the freeze-thaw cycles so hard on plants. This will provide less protection and in spring the soil will generally be damper. No matter where you live in a city, it will be slightly milder than the surrounding countryside which explains why there are frost-warnings for suburbs before there are for downtown. Buildings act as a radiator of heat as do all other forms of concrete and glass.

ELEVATION ❧ The higher you are, the lower the temperatures and the more precipitation you can expect. For every 330 feet (100 meters) there's a drop of 1°F (.5°C) in temperature. Wind force increases as you go higher.

MARINE INFLUENCE ❧ Water modifies the temperature of the surrounding land. It's warmer in winter and cooler in summer. This may affect an area several miles (kilometers) inland and will extend frost-free days. When moist air hits rising land, it cools and falls as rain or snow. In low lying areas there will be less precipitation. Inland lakes and rivers heat the surrounding air which absorbs large amounts of moisture. When it cools, fog forms. This inhibits frost and extends the frost-free season.

(Zone 9) Saxe Point Park is a rarity—a public park filled with perennials. Designed by George Radford, the gardens must endure winds gusting off the sea: LIMNANTHES DOUGLASII; GENISTA; CAMPANULA.

WIND ❧ Winds add an extraordinary drying factor as well as a cooling effect. Wind breaks will increase the snow cover. And snow cover is one of the best mulches there is.

Frost dates in any area may vary by weeks because of differences in local conditions. You can note it in your gardening diary or phone your local agricultural station for up-to-date information.

Find your over-all hardiness zone on the map on page 134. All the plants mentioned up to and including that zone will work for you. For instance, if you live in Zone 5, you can use all the plants in Zones 2, 3, 4 *and* 5. With winter protection you might be able to keep plants from Zone 6 alive in some parts of your garden.

The growing season starts on the day in spring

*David Tomlinson grows plants that aren't supposed to thrive in **Zone 5**.*
His garden (Merlin's Hollow) is an area of experimentation. From top left: DELPHINIUM;
MALVA MOSCHATA, *Musk Mallow;* ACHILLEA, *Yarrow, Moonshine;* DIANTHUS, *Rainbow loveliness;*
SEDUM SPECTABILIS, *Showy Stonecrop;* IRIS PUMILA, *Dwarf Bearded Iris;* PENSTEMON SMALLII,
Beard-tongue; IRIS GERMANICA, *Bearded Iris;* STACHYS MACRANTHA, *Woundwort;* TRADESCANTIA
ANDERSONIANA, *Spiderwort;* THALICTRUM HYBRIDA, *Meadow Rue;* LYSIMACHIA PUNCTATA, *Loosestrife;*
MACLEAYA MICROCARPA, *Plume Poppy;* PAEONIA, *Sarah Bernhardt;* PYRETHRUM, *Painted Daisy;*
OENOTHERA FRUTICOSA, *Evening Primrose;* PAEONIA FESTIVA MAXIMA; STACHYS OLYMPICA, *Lamb's-ears.*

when the average temperature reaches 41°F (5°C)—the daily maximum will reach 50°F (10°C) with a minimum of 32°F (0°C). If you want to figure this out for yourself, temperatures in professional weather stations are usually taken 3.9 feet (1.2 meters) above ground; or 1 to 2 inches (3 to 4 centimeters) above short grass to get crop temperature. On clear nights the minimum grass temperature is lower than on a cloudy night. After sunset the ground cools rapidly. If there is no wind the air will be cooler; a light wind will mix warm surface air and cooler ground air.

NUMBER OF GROWING DAYS
IN EACH ZONE

Zone 1: 100 days
     2: 150 days
     3: 165 days
     4: 195 days
     5: 210 days
     6: 225 days
     7: 255 days
     8: 270 days
     9: 330 days

As you can see, in the higher zones there is a much longer growing season, and usually a much warmer winter. What most zone maps don't take into account, unfortunately, is the height you are above sea level. So that Zone 4 on the East coast is not going to be the same as Zone 4 in the Rockies or in Quebec. Each region will have its own characteristics. And these can change from year to year depending on how much snow cover and rain you've been blessed with.

YOUR MICROCLIMATE

I happen to live in Zone 6. But my garden has spots that are a cooler Zone 5 beneath a north-facing fence which holds frost and snow longer than anywhere else in the garden. And then a warmer Zone 7 in front of a south-facing fence that gets sun most of the day. It's also protected from the icy winter blasts out of the north. These microclimates will nurture different plants than other parts of the garden.

To work out your microclimate observe your garden over a year or two. Start thinking about the general climate of your area, then work back to specifics. Your immediate neighborhood might have many different microclimates. And the microclimate of your garden will have a number of factors that provide its special conditions, depending on location and all the different elements found in it. For instance:

❦ The size and number of existing trees. This is important since they draw water from deep in the earth and cool the air around them.

❦ How much shade the trees cast. Look at where the heaviest shadows fall each week (every day if you have the patience) and calculate how many hours of sun each section gets. And keep in mind that this will change as the season advances. The sun will of course get lower in the sky as fall approaches.

❦ A light colored fence will reflect more light and retain heat, warming and drying the soil nearby. If you plant bulbs in front of it, you'll have the earliest spring showing along that stretch.

❦ How damp the soil is and how much moisture it retains.

❦ The prevailing winds, especially if they come from the north and bring arctic air with them, or off a large body of water on a regular basis.

Then work on the microclimate or mini-zones in your own garden. Put thermometers near fences, under the canopies of any existing trees, out in open spaces.

❧ Check on where the winds come from and when (you don't plant tall plants in an area where the north wind hits them in June).

❧ Calculate the number of hours of sun you get each day in each area by dividing up the garden into sections easily worked out by eye. Is there an area that's partly shady, say near a southern fence? Another under the branches of two trees? Another with no cover at all near a northern fence? Each section will have its own demands.

Kinds of shade:

Partial—sun comes into this part of the garden for a few hours each day.

Dappled—sun penetrates through leaves of a high branched tree.

Deep—rarely gets sun.

Kinds of sun:

Partial—3 - 5 hours

Full—a minimum of 6 hours

Seek out plants that appreciate conditions similar to your garden. Don't put a full sun plant into deep shade; nor a bog plant in a dry poor soil—not if you want them to thrive. And don't leave a plant happiest in a higher zone without some sort of winter protection. The most sensible approach is to put plants with similar backgrounds together—desert plants with desert plants for instance; and try to replicate their original habitat.

By knowing something about your zone and all the potential zones in your microclimate, you will have a great deal of latitude in what you can plant.

You might have as much as a three-zone sweep with the potential for far more interesting plant selection than that most commonly available.

THE GREENHOUSE EFFECT ON YOUR GARDEN

The greenhouse effect: The holding down of warmer air by the ozone; holes in the ozone that let scorching ultraviolet rays of the sun pour through; temperature inversions. These have all become frightening realities in the past few years. Because of pollution from cars and hydro-fluorocarbon wastes, this warming trend will inevitably have an effect on the garden. There may be longer periods of drought in areas where the norm has been a seven-year cycle on, seven-year off. The intensity of the sun's rays may increase.

You can help in a small way by not using deadly sprays in any form. But equally as important is to work with this climate change—use plants that are drought resistant and therefore require less water. Put in sophisticated new methods of drip irrigation to cut down on evaporation. Water gets to the roots more readily, unlike the old fountain types which allowed profligate evaporation. Recycle as much of your kitchen and garden waste as possible through composting.

PLANT LISTINGS

Think of your garden as a kind of laboratory where you are always experimenting. As you become more experienced, your taste will change. You'll lust after different kinds of plants and plantings. On the previous pages we looked at different styles of gardens. You can try any of these anywhere in the country.

My favorite perennials are described in more detail. They're also the ones I've worked with. Most of them are extremely hardy and tolerant of some drying out. If they aren't, I've pointed that out. An "x" in the Listings indicates a hybrid.

You can create almost any kind of a garden you want but the most important factor to keep in mind is to work with what you've got—work with nature rather than against it. Growing a lawn in the desert is just as foolish and heartbreaking as trying to create an English cottage garden in the Arctic. Let your site inform you and you'll be a much happier gardener. Then let your imagination run wild.

*(**Zone 5**) Betty Piper's garden by the sea is a refreshing combination of old-fashioned flowers:*
Daylily; ASTILBE; GAILLARDIA; DELPHINIUM.
In the foreground: wild CAMPANULA; *Dwarf* GERANIUM; *Pink* PYRETHRUM; ARTEMISIA, *Silver King.*

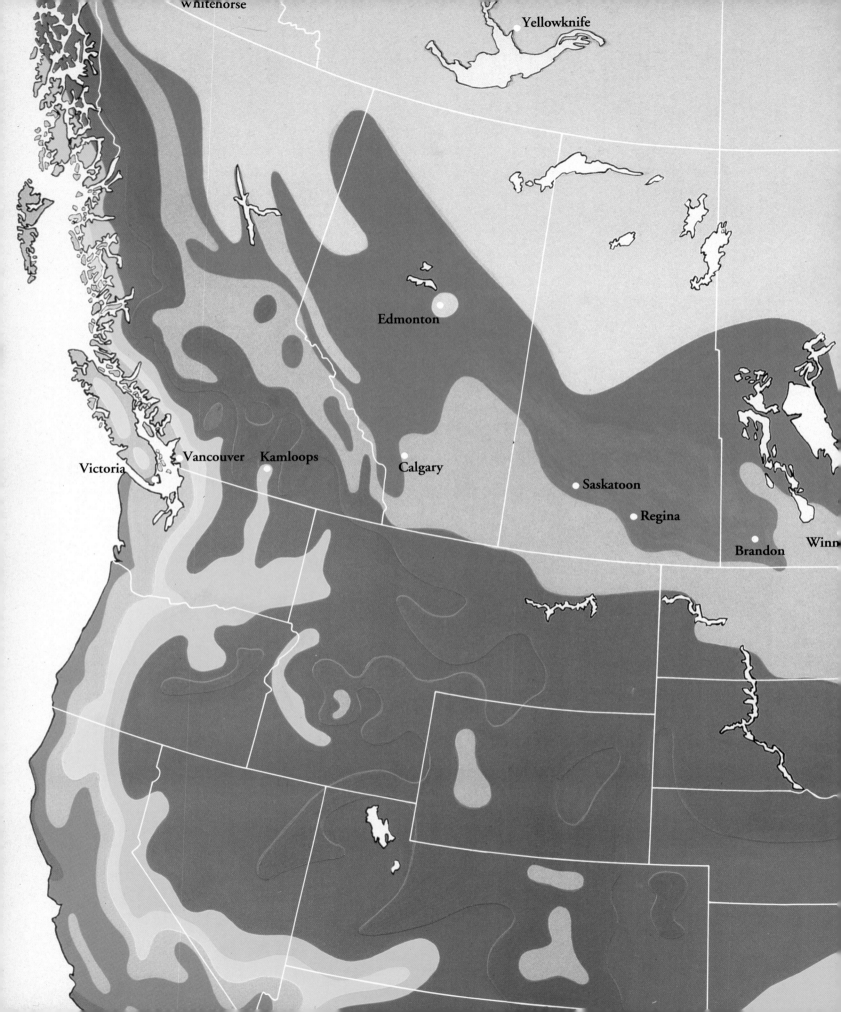

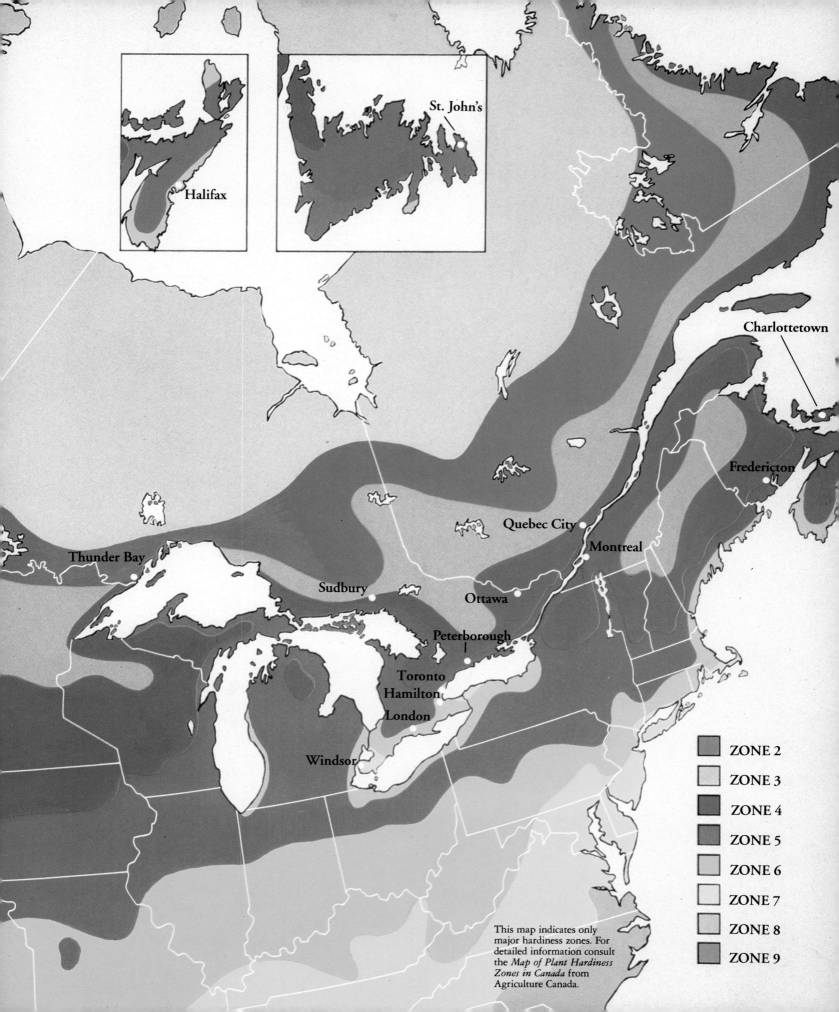

St. John's

Halifax

Charlottetown

Fredericton

Quebec City

Montreal

Thunder Bay

Sudbury

Ottawa

Peterborough

Toronto
Hamilton
London

Windsor

ZONE 2
ZONE 3
ZONE 4
ZONE 5
ZONE 6
ZONE 7
ZONE 8
ZONE 9

This map indicates only major hardiness zones. For detailed information consult the *Map of Plant Hardiness Zones in Canada* from Agriculture Canada.

HARDINESS ZONES
TWO AND THREE

North to people who live in the northern part of North America can be as far north as the Arctic Circle. Zones two and three blanket a fascinating range of habitats. Plants have evolved there to survive in the wildest, most devastating winters, devoid of moisture except for snowfall. Then comes the brief spring and a glory hard to describe to anyone who hasn't lived in any of the Norths. One day nothing seems to be happening. The next, woods and fields are crowned with a magnificent spectacle of blooms. What is most hardy, it appears, is also the most extravagant in the color spectrum.

In zone 1 and most northerly parts of 2 the days can be as long as 20 hours each which makes up for the shorter season and the reason why there is such a burst of color once the season gets going.

Anyone gardening in the very far north must become intimate with the native population of plants. Many plants have been taken from the wild and domesticated for the rest of the continent. But here there are possibilities quite different from anywhere else. ARCTOSTAPHYLOS UVA-URSI, Kinikinik, is a native ground cover that grows right up to the Arctic Circle. It has rich green foliage and bright red berries. It can grow just about anywhere in the country but is particularly valuable in more northern climate zones because of its adaptability to severe temperatures.

CLIMATIC CONSIDERATIONS:
Minimum temperatures run from -50°F (-45°C) in zone 1 to -40°F (-40°C) in zone 3.
Zone 1 has approximately 100 growing days; zone 2, 150 growing days;
zone 3, 165 growing days.

Indicator shrubs:
Zone 1: AMELANCHIER ALNIFOLIA, Saskatoonberry, in the West (Shadbush in the East); COTONEASTER LUCIDA, Hedge Cotoneaster; PINUS MUGO MUGHUS, Mugo Pine.
Zone 2: CARAGANA ARBORESCENS, Siberian Pea Shrub; CORNUS ALBA 'SIBIRICA', Siberian Dogwood; COTONEASTER INTEGERRIMUS, European Cotoneaster.
Zone 3: EUONYMUS ALATA, Winged Spindle Tree; RHUS TYPHINA, Staghorn Sumac; SPIRAEA X ARGUTA, Garland Spirea.
These plants indicate what will grow at the edge of a zone and will give you more information about hardiness in your area.

(Zone 8) Kathie Leishmann has radiant spots everywhere in her garden.
Here is native IRIS PSEUDACORUS fronted by ACONITUM 'Ivorine' and PINACAE.

It is so useful and attractive that the Botanical Gardens of the University of British Columbia has introduced a cultivar that does well in warmer climates—A. VANCOUVER JADE.

Many ornamentals, grasses, evergreens and flowering shrubs grow better in the north than in the south especially in areas where there is good snow cover and little freeze-thaw to contend with.

Ornamental shrubs such as lilac, crabapple, hydrangea, honeysuckle, mock orange, viburnum and shrub roses do brilliantly here. And nowhere else are delphiniums quite so magnificent. Because they die to the ground in winter, perennials have automatic root protection. This means they are not only hardy but a great group of plants to cultivate.

Keep in mind some of the other climatic facts of life:

❧ Cold northern and westerly winds blowing across the garden can keep it from warming in spring. It can also dry out evergreens. Tie evergreen boughs with a strong rope or make tents of burlap open top and bottom for air circulation; construct board shelters of laths. Don't use plastic because it acts like a greenhouse and could raise the temperature around the plant high enough to break dormancy.

❧ The sun can scald plants even in winter: the temperature of bark heats up in sunshine and when there's a sudden dip on the thermometer, moisture freezes and the bark splits. Protect shrubs with blankets of burlap.

❧ Midwinter thaws and phenomena, such as the chinook that affects parts of Alberta: sky-rocketing temperatures melt the snow and fool plants into thinking spring is here.

Then it plunges again. These freeze-thaw swings are disastrous to all plants except those that have adapted to these fluctuations. Once again check on the plants native to your area.

❧ Wind transporting cool air from the Arctic can also bring with it day after day of clear sunshine—even so it's not wise to put in plants that love extreme heat.

❧ Gardens facing southeast catching the warm morning rays of the sun will flourish most readily.

❧ Hilltops are a bad location for the garden. Winds keep the soil cool; part way up a hill is best since cool air will settle in a valley and warm air rises. Choose a spot where trees and buildings won't cut off the sun for part of the day. And don't block cool air from flowing downward by putting in a windbreak below your slope.

❧ Snow offers protection and a form of insulation for plants but if it drifts too high the weight will crush small shrubs and trees. If you can, keep the tops cleared. Build wooden tepees or tie up evergreens that might be hard hit.

❧ Windbreaks will slow down killer winds and help pile up drifting snow for winter protection. Evergreens of course are the most useful trees and, in the north, the most attractive.

I remember living in Northern Alberta as a child and, during spring, seeing bed sheets thrown over gardens to protect precious vegetables. It's still a good method if there's a frost warning in late spring—put them out in the afternoon to keep in some of that day's heat. And take off the protector in the morning.

In starting a new border, spread a sheet of plastic over the bed for a couple of days to speed up the heating of the soil. If there are weed seeds

*(**Zone 6**) Murray Haig created this raised bed from construction leftovers. He experiments with color in this area, and changes the plants three times a year. Pansies in transition; purple* SALVIA; *trailing* GERANIUM; *sunshine* IMPATIENS; *pink hybrid* BEGONIA; SEDUM; *left:* LIATRIS *(not in flower but they are purple and white);* RUDBECKIA, *purple Coneflower;* CALADIUM, *variegated foliage. In the background is* ROGERSIA, DICENTRA LUXURIANTE. *In front:* ACHILLEA, *Cerise Queen.*

lurking around they will be forced to show themselves. Pick them out. The earth will be warmed up enough to plant.

You might want to consider raised beds since they warm up faster and drain better than anything at ground level and can raise the temperature of the soil by 5°F (2.2°C). Raise the soil at least 6 inches (15 centimeters) and hold it in place with bricks, stones, boards, or railway ties to keep the soil from running off when you water. One of the cleverest raised beds I've seen was built because the designer of the garden had no place in which to put a lot of blocks of concrete left over from construction. He dug down, used all these chunks as drainage and built up the soil on top. See above.

SOIL ❧ Soil varies from one side of the continent to the other but south of the tundra (a damp spongy peat) it tends to be on the sandy side. This means drainage is good, sometimes too good, and the addition of peat moss will help reduce nutrient loss. Northern gardeners suggest using fish planted below the soil as manure. This is an ancient practice and there is no reason to abandon it. Jackfish or any other bony fish that's readily available can be used. The generally accepted soil combination in the North is 2 parts peat to 1 part sand. The marvellous Devonian Botanical Gardens just outside Edmonton are all planted in this mixture and the range of plants they grow is astonishing. Liming of soils, especially those most heavily acidic, stretches the kinds of plants you can use—add calcium carbonate. Do this anyway if your foliage turns yellow in midseason.

When you are buying plants in any of these zones get them early enough in the season to make sure they'll put down sturdy roots before the onslaught of the first frost. In the Eastern Arctic you'll have to think seriously of putting in gro-lights or even a small greenhouse to stretch your season. Elsewhere cold or hot frames are indispensable. You can prolong the season for up to 60 days by starting seeds indoors in March, moving them out to cold frames when the days get longer and hardening them off before planting in the garden proper. It's also the place where you can overwinter woody cuttings from shrubs and perennials. A hot frame with soil-warming cables beneath it will broaden your scope even more. Cloches, plastic plant covers, can also be season extenders.

PLANT MAINTENANCE ❧ Cut tops off perennials at 6 inches (15 centimeters) from soil level. Cover with evergreen branches. Roses especially need this treatment. Use a mulch over bulbs, then cover with branches to hold it down. One of the joys of northern gardening is that there aren't the usual plagues of pests. But make sure you check plants thoroughly when bringing them in from the South. Shear evergreens in late spring—a light shave on the outside will stimulate growth in the interior.

WINTER MAINTENANCE ❧ Adjust to your own microclimate rather than the general one. You'll be surprised and pleased with the results.

Don't be too scrupulous about cleaning up your garden in the fall. Bend the stalks of tall plants in to cover up the crown and give them the greatest protection possible. In spring you'll find that the stalks come out easily. Be sure to reread the section on mulch and compost (see page 50) and once you've had a good frost apply winter mulch.

(Zone 3) David Harrop built a luxurious garden in the north where the temperature can drop to -40°. He grows hardy plants, DELPHINIUM, for instance, that will survive the harsh climate. From left to right: ROSA RUGOSA, shrub rose 'Therese Bugnet'; HEMEROCALLIS; HOSTA FORTUNEI; Standard (Tree Rose) Hybrid Tea; GEUM URBANUM SIBIRICUM; AQUILEGIA; CHRYSANTHEMUM LEUCANTHEMUM, Ox-eye Daisy.

SELECTED LISTINGS FOR
HARDINESS ZONES TWO AND THREE

ACHILLEA (a-kill-EE-a) 🌿 **Yarrow**
A dependable, pleasantly aromatic perennial that thrives under the worst of conditions. It has feathery, fernlike foliage; is excellent for cutting and drying.

Uses: Depending on variety they can be used for borders or rock gardens. Although they make excellent dried flower arrangements, you can keep the flowers cut back and simply enjoy the feathery foliage. It can add tension to a border that consists mainly of erect stems.

Maintenance: Keep deadheading for more blooms; all forms can be invasive so keep pulling out off-shoots, dividing to keep a good shape; propagates easily by root division, which is best done in midsummer every 2 to 3 years. Cut back to 4" (10 cm) in the fall.

Light: Full sun.

Size: 8" - 48" (20 cm - 120 cm) high, 12" - 36" (30 cm - 90 cm) wide.

Color: Ranges from pale yellow to salmon to deep red rose and white. The foliage has a fernlike effect in most; the A. FILIPENDULA has a more frondy appearance. A. F. 'MOONBEAM' is a favorite.

Blooms: June to September.

Soil: Thrives in poor, well-drained soils that are not heavy or wet.

Watering: Drought resistant.

Origin: Europe and Asia.

ACONITUM NAPELLUS
(ak-o-NY-tum) 🌿 **Monkshood**
A showy, easy to care for perennial

herb whose parts are poisonous, although the tuberous root was often used as a topical treatment for rheumatism. Don't try it.

Uses: Substitute for delphinium, which it closely resembles, in shaded spots. Thrives in moist, even marshy areas. Also combines well with ferns, thalictrum, Japanese anemone, astilbe, and hostas.

Maintenance: Difficult to establish in warm, dry places. Plant 15-18 inches (40-45 centimeters) apart in spring, mulch annually in late spring and cut back to soil level in fall. Roots do not like to be disturbed but need division in the fall every 3 to 4 years. Also propagate by seed. Never plant them where children play, near vegetable gardens or any other places where they may be inadvertently eaten.

Light: Partial shade, will tolerate full sun in northern locations.

Size: 24" - 72" (60 cm - 180 cm) high, 18" - 24" (45 cm - 60 cm) wide.

Color: Hood or helmet-shaped blossoms have a mysterious almost threatening look to them: blue, violet blue, lilac to white, yellow or cream.

Blooms: August to October.

Soil: Easy to grow in fertile, cool, moisture-retentive soil. Some will thrive in boggy or marshy soil.

Watering: Keep well watered.

Origin: Europe and Asia.

ALCHEMILLA MOLLIS
(al-kem-ILL-a) 🌿 **Lady's-mantle**
A popular herbaceous perennial,

commonly found in English gardens. It was originally supposed to play a part in alchemy, hence its name. This is one of my favorite plants. It will hold the last drop of dew in its saucer-like leaves. Another touch of magic.

Uses: Harmonizes well with other plants, makes a good ground cover and is excellent for cut flower arrangements; use it under shrubs; as a hedge; plant it with almost anything, or in a special area on its own. One of the most practical perennials in the garden.

Maintenance: Propagate by division in fall or seed in spring. It can get out of control so be sure to deadhead if you want to contain it. Don't be surprised if you find seedlings everywhere. I don't think you can have too many of these plants anyway.

Light: Full sun, partial shade in hot areas.

Size: 12" (30 cm) high, 18" (45 cm) wide in sprawling clumps.

Color: Beautiful foliage plant with downy, grey-green, scalloped leaves. Blooms, almost acid green, are in fluted dense clusters above the leaves.

Blooms: May to June.

Soil: Well-drained but moist soil.

Watering: Keep well watered.

Origin: Europe.

ALLIUM CAERULEUM (AL-ium)
🌿 **Blue Globe Onion**
Allium is a huge family of bulbs—onion, leek, garlic—and you'll find different ones in all zones.

*(**Zone 5**) At the front of Amy Stewart's border is* ACHEMILLA MOLLIS, *Lady's-mantle mixed with* SPIRAEA X ARUNDSII ALBA; *right:* CORYDALIS LUTEA. *The border is tied together with drifts of* ALCHEMILLA, BERGENIA, *Siberian Iris,* EUPHORBIA MYRSINITES, *Myrtle spurge.*

There are so many kinds of ornamental alliums, try almost any of them. They go from the A. GIGANTEUM which really is huge, down to tiny little jewel-like creatures.

Uses: Because of the very slender stems you can interplant them throughout the garden; mass them for another kind of effect; associate them with other plants the same size so that the fading stems and seed heads won't look unsightly; try very small ones in the rock garden.

Maintenance: Divide overgrown clumps in spring or fall; plant bulbs in early to mid-fall, or as soon as available, in well-drained soil three times the depth of the bulbs (in the north plant at least 6 inches [15 centimeters] deep). Lift and divide every three years. Fertilize in spring and watch out for slugs which love them.

Light: Full sun.

Size: 4" - 48" (10 cm - 120 cm) high, 3" - 12" (8 cm - 30 cm) wide.

Color: From a pure white to pink, yellow and deep purple.

Blooms: June.

Soil: Any kind of well-drained soil.

Watering: Keep well-watered.

Origin: Mediterranean.

Other alliums to look for: A. MOLY, Golden Garlic; A. CERNUM, Rose Flower; A. ÐOUGLASII will take winter and wet soils of the Columbia plateau; A. OREOPHILUM or A. OSTROW-SKIANUM (Zone 5); A. GIGANTEUM (Zone 5), 4 feet (1.2 meters); A. KARATAVIENSE (Zone 5) white; A.

TUBEROSUM (Zone 4), Garlic Chives, is a wonderful fragrant white cut flower.

ANTHEMIS TINCTORIA KELWAYI (AN-them-is) ❧ **Golden Marguerite**
One of the best of the perennial daisies. I like it for the silvery scented foliage as well as for the little yellow flowers. This cultivar has particularly bright lemon yellow flowers.

Uses: Long-lasting blooms make excellent cut flowers; it's great as a filler among larger more dense plants.

Maintenance: Tends to have mildew in areas of poor air circulation. This plant can be messy if you don't have it in a contained place. It produces masses of flowers and almost kills itself with the effort; keep deadheading and cut back sections to the base to promote healthy growth. Propagate by rooting basal shoots, or seed, or by division in fall or spring.

Light: Full sun.

Size: 18" - 36" (45 cm - 90 cm) high, 36" (90 cm) wide.

Color: Bright yellow florets and silver-green foliage.

Blooms: June to September.

Soil: Prefers a slightly alkaline, dry soil.

Watering: Average water needs.

Origin: Central and southern Europe and Asia.

AQUILEGIA CANADENSIS (ak-wil-EE-jia) ❧ **Wild Columbine**
This is a woodland perennial related to the buttercup. It's been part of traditional cottage gardens for hundreds of years and attracts hummingbirds.

Uses: Lovely foliage makes this a light airy plant with an extra long season and cheerful flowers. There are many kinds suitable for every part of the country.

A. ALPINA is suitable for the natural garden. A. CANADENSIS is a native plant. A. MCKANA GIANT is a long-spurred hybrid.

Maintenance: Deadhead constantly and the flowers will keep on coming back. They are great little self-seeders but the seedlings rarely come up true—that is, they don't look like the parent plant. To propagate: plant seeds in spring or divide in dormant season. Replace old plants every 3 years. Subject to leaf miner.

Light: Full sun in mild climates, partial shade elsewhere.

Size: 12" - 36" (30 cm - 90 cm) high, 6" - 12" (15 cm -30 cm) wide.

Color: Spurred blooms range from delicate pastel hues, to blue, mixes of red-yellow and white. Fresh green, divided leaves are reminiscent of maidenhair ferns.

Blooms: Spring to early summer.

Soil: Thrives in good, loamy well-drained soil.

Watering: Keep moist.

Origin: Europe, Asia, North America.

ARABIS CAUCASICA (AR-a-bis) ❧ **Wall Rock Cress**
Herbaceous perennial of the mustard family, this rockery plant is valued for its mat or tuftlike year-round foliage which throws up loose clusters of fragrant flowers.

Uses: Great for the rockery and for pattern planting, as an edging or for planting over spring flowering bulbs such as daffodils and narcissi—covers up a multitude of sins.

Maintenance: Shear flowers back to stalk after blooms are spent or it becomes terribly straggly. You can almost pull them out by hand—experiment but don't cut the foliage back. Spread around almost any time during the season by taking a group of rosettes and replanting them.

Light: Full sun.

Size: 6" - 12" (15 cm - 30 cm) high, 12" - 24" (30 cm - 60 cm) wide.

Color: Chalk white to rosy pink flowers almost smother the attractive grey-green foliage in spring. Look for the variegated version—a great foliage plant.

Blooms: April to May.

Soil: Does best in somewhat lean, limy well-drained soil.

Watering: Moderate.

Origin: Southern Europe, Asia Minor, Caucasus, North America.

ARTEMISIA (ART-e-mesia) ❧ **Ghost Plant, Sagebrush, Wormwood**
This is a huge and confusing family all with beautiful silvery foliage and dozens of common names from Dusty-miller to Old-woman. Get as many as you have room for.

Uses: As a foil for almost any plant in the garden since the foliage ranges from a soft feathery grey-green to a fine white leather; for massing or as a thread running through the garden drawing the eye along it; absolutely a perfect companion to any blue or purple flower; it will cool down very strong tones.

Maintenance: Keep clipping and shaping 'Silver Mound' or it will fall into the center; keep in check by pulling out or cutting back regularly. Easy to propagate by division just about any time.

Light: Like all silver foliage plants lots of sun.

Size: 24" - 60" (60 cm - 150 cm) high, 24" (60 cm) wide.

Blooms: Insignificant since this is a foliage plant that's good for three seasons; looks a bit scraggly in winter.

ARTEMISIA LUDOVICIANA is Western Sagebrush; A. DRACUNCULUS is French Tarragon. My favorites are A. 'Lambrook Silver', A.L. VAR.

ALBULA 'Silver King', A. 'Silver Queen' and A. 'DISCOLOR'. A. SCHMIDTIANA 'Silver Mound' also has a dwarf form called 'NANA' which is small enough for the rock garden. A. STELLERANA is excellent for planting by the sea.

Soil: Thrives in poor dry soil.
Watering: Drought resistant.

Origin: Europe, North America.

ARUNCUS SYLVESTER
(a-RUNK-us) ❧ **Goatsbeard**
A hardy, shrublike perennial related to the rose family. The sexes are separate: the male with the staminate flowers makes the showier display.
Uses: Because of its height it is best

used at the rear of a perennial border.
Maintenance: Virtually trouble-free once it's established, it can be propagated by seed or division.
Light: Full sun; partial shade.
Size: 4' to 7' (120 cm - 210 cm) high, 3' (90 cm) wide.
Color: A large show of tiny white flowers massed on the panicles of the

*(**Zone 6**) Serenity dominates J. Schofield Manuel's garden designed by Murray Haig: Sunshine* IMPATIENS *in the pot; back:* COTONEASTER DAMMERI; ARTEMISIA *Silver Mound;* ROSA, *The Fairy;* EUONYMUS *Emerald Gaiety; beneath the wall covered with Boston Ivy is* ARTEMISIA *Silver King.*

(Zone 5) Amy Stewart planted this gorgeous combination:
CAMPANULA PERSICIFOLIA 'ALBA', *Bellflower; and* DELPHINIUM.

male plant—they look a bit like the feathery Blooms of Astilbe.

Blooms: June to July.
Soil: Rich, moist soil.
Watering: Keep well watered.
Origin: North America.

ASTER NOVI-BELGII (AS-ter)
❧ **Michaelmas Daisy**
One of a large group of perennial wild flowers, this is just about my favorite for the late summer and fall garden. Looks good not only in formal gardens but also in native and wild gardens.

Uses: Use behind more modest perennials or among shrubs; it comes into its own when most of the garden is beginning to fade; good cut flower.

Maintenance: Resistant to disease except mildew so keep it where there is good air circulation; fertilize sparingly to avoid soft, rank, disease-prone growth; pinch young shoots at about 6 inches (15 centimeters), except where the season is short, and then later to encourage bushy growth. Propagate by division in spring or fall every two years to control any predilection for invasiveness, but it's so easy to layer I usually go that route (see page 43). It will also self-seed.

Light: Full sun.

Size: 12" - 48" (30 cm - 120 cm) high, 18" (45 cm) wide.

Color: Full clusters of 1-inch (2-centimeter), bright blue-violet flowers. Other varieties range from white through the pinks to purple.

Blooms: September to October.

Soil: Moist, fertile soils.

Watering: More luxuriant with regular watering. Water well during dry spells; hand water—hates getting its foliage wet.

Origin: North America, Asia, Europe.

Baby's-breath *see* GYPSOPHILA PANICULATA

BAPTISIA AUSTRALIS (bap-TIZ-ia) ⅍ **False Indigo**

These handsome relatives of the pea family have great ornamental value with pealike blooms arranged up and down the fleshy stem.

Uses: Holds up well in bouquets, clumps of the bush make a great addition to the natural or wild garden because of low maintenance requirements.

Maintenance: Deadhead; doesn't like roots disturbed—I moved mine and it took ages to come back. Propagate by division before or after blooming time. May need staking.

Light: Full sun, partial shade.

Size: 3'- 6' (90 cm - 180 cm) high, 3' (90 cm) wide.

Color: Foliage is a rich bluish green with blue flowers resembling the sweet pea.

Blooms: May to June. Or later in northern gardens.

Soil: Ordinary soil but dislikes lime.

Watering: Drought resistant.

Origin: Eastern United States.

Beard-tongue *see* PENSTEMON BARBATUS

BERGENIA CORDIFOLIA (Ber-GEN-ia) ⅍ **Heartleaf Bergenia**

One of the most valuable of all the shade plants, a ground cover prized for foliage and flower. This is not to everyone's taste. Some find the size rather vulgar. I don't.

Uses: Excellent ground cover along paths or under shrubs and trees. It provides winter color since even the luscious leaves stay green if there's snow protection. Leaves used by florists.

Maintenance: Leave plants undisturbed. Only remove flower stems after blooming. When it gets crowded, divide it either in fall or spring.

Light: Partial shade.

Size: 18" - 24" (45 cm - 60 cm) high, 24" (60 cm) wide.

Color: The bold almost leathery leaves are shaped like elephant's ears with clusters of waxy flowers on strong stems. Rosy red bloom.

Blooms: Spring.

Soil: Tolerant of wide range of soil but not of too rich a diet. This will encourage leafy growth at the expense of blooms.

Watering: Keep moist; will grow more slowly in dry soil.

Origin: Siberia.

Blazing Star *see* LIATRIS SPICATA

Bleeding Heart *see* DICENTRA SPECTABILIS

Blue Globe Onion *see* ALLIUM CAERULEUM

CAMPANULA POSCHARSKYANA (kam-PAN-ew-la) ⅍ **Serbian Bellflower**

I'd like every campanula to be in my garden. I've singled this one out

because it's a good starter plant and needs little work for lots of blooms. Its hardiness enables it to be used in places as varied as walls and banks of pools.

Uses: Can be used in a shaded border near pools, in dry walls; as a trailing plant on a rock wall; or as a ground cover.

Maintenance: Easy to please; plant in early fall or late spring. Deadhead after flowering to encourage new blooms. Easily propagated by division in fall or spring.

Light: Full sun, light shade in hot climates.

Size: Plant spreads to 18" (45 cm). Although stems may be as long as 2' (60 cm), they trail over the ground and usually reach a height of only 6" (15 cm).

Color: Lavender-blue.

Blooms: June to July.

Soil: Well-drained, fertile, preferably neutral to alkaline.

Watering: Drought resistant.

Origin: Europe.

C. LACTIFLORA has a white flower on a stalk that grows to 4' (120 cm).

C. CARPATICA 'Blue Clips' is suitable for the rockery.

Catmint *see* NEPETA

CERASTIUM TOMENTOSUM (ser-ASS-tium) ⅍ **Snow-in-summer**

A low-growing plant that performs well anywhere, including coastal or desert climates. I like its greyish, woolly foliage.

Uses: Ground cover on sunny banks, or in rock gardens. Can be used along paths or driveways. Will cascade over walls; good container plant since it runs rampant—combine with cobalt blue lobelia. Because it will cover a fairly large area in a short time it's a good filler—you'll probably end up having to keep it contained.

Maintenance: A light shear after flowering for neatness. Propagates by seed which are viable in soil for several years and therefore it can be a pest. Divide in fall or early spring.
Light: Full sun.
Size: Plant forms a dense mat with 6" (15 cm) to 12" (30 cm) high stems, can spread up to 3' (90cm) in one year.
Color: Fuzzy, grey foliage with intense white blooms clustered on stems.
Blooms: June.
Soil: Very adaptable, will even grow in pure sand. Good drainage is the only requirement.
Watering: Drought resistant, standing water will cause root rot.
Origin: Europe.

CHIONODOXA LUCILIAE
(ky-o-no-DOX-a) ❧ **Glory-of-the-snow**
This charming little bulb, belonging to the lily family, is one of the first to bloom in the spring. Its origin is alpine meadows.
Uses: Best for a sunny rock garden.
Maintenance: Propagation by seed and offsets. Plant bulbs 3 inches (7.5 centimeters) deep in September or October. May have to be renewed every few years.
Light: Full sun.
Size: 6" (15 cm) high, 4" (10 cm) wide.
Color: Blue or white.
Blooms: Early spring.
Soil: Does well in rockeries, well-drained sites.
Watering: Give plenty of moisture.
Origin: Crete, Asia Minor.

Christmas Rose *see* HELLEBORUS NIGER

Coralbells *see* HEUCHERA CANADENSIS

Daylily *see* HEMEROCALLIS

DELPHINIUM ELATUM
(del-FIN-ium) ❧ **Larkspur**
One of the greatest of all traditional plants—elegant, stately—no garden should be without several of them.
Uses: Plant for height and spectacular effect. When it's combined with the Madonna or any other white lily, the result is especially dramatic in the early June garden.
Maintenance: Grows best in cooler areas. Plant in fall or early spring in a site sheltered from winds, otherwise they will need staking with thin canes which should be installed before the plant gets too big. Cut back after first bloom; when new growth emerges allow only three or four stalks to grow—this will promote a second blooming. You may have to replace them every five years or so. There are places on the east coast, however, that have plants 25 years old.
Light: Needs at least a half day of sun, but prefers full sun.
Size: 3' - 8' (1 m - 2.5 m) high, 12" - 36" (30 cm - 90 cm) wide.
Color: Comes in true cobalt blue—very rare in plant colors—and ranges from white to yellow, pink, purple and red. Large flat flower has contrasting eye. There are many 'Pacific' hybrids including: Black Knight (dark blue), Galahad (white), King Arthur (violet), Connecticut Yankee (mixed colors); D. NUDICAULE is scarlet.
Blooms: June and may come again in August when cut back.
Soil: Deep, rich, moist, porous soil. Add lime to strongly acidic soil.
Watering: Keep well watered.
Origin: North America, Europe.

DIANTHUS DELTOIDES
(dy-AN-thus) ❧ **Maiden Pink, Pinks**
Pinks grow in grasslike clumps with pleasantly scented flowers rising above grey-green leaves—almost worth growing them for the foliage alone. I'd like to adopt all of this family.
Uses: To decorate the front of herbaceous borders, to edge beds, and add variety to rock gardens. Alpine types do well in walls, rockeries. Many hybrids are grown for cut flowers, particularly the D. CARYOPHYLLUS, Carnation; D. DELTOIDES COCCINEUS is a very satisfying rather brilliant ground cover.
D. PLUMARIUS is the true old-fashioned cottage pink valued for its scent and hardiness.
Maintenance: Pinks lose their vigor after a couple of growing seasons and need replacement. Propagation from seed or stem cuttings (take cuttings of vegetative shoots in growing season and root in moist, shaded soil). Cut back after blooming for new flowers. Mulch with boughs after the ground freezes in cold areas; the ground covers need to have dead flowerheads pulled out with a flick of the wrist—with this action a lot of the dead stuff underneath comes away—good for the plant.
Light: Full sun.
Size: 6" - 24" (15 cm - 60 cm) high, 8" - 24" (20 cm -60 cm) wide.
Color: White through the pinks to deep reds, in single or double blooms with hummocks of evergreen, grasslike leaves of a grey-green.
Blooms: Late spring, with some blooming into early fall.
Soil: A well-drained alkaline sandy loam is best.
Watering: Don't let them dry out because they don't do well under hot, dry conditions.
Origin: Ranges from Siberia, to South Africa and Asia.

(Zone 5) Midge Ellis Keeble's DELPHINIUM, *Pacific Giant Galahad strain were raised easily from seed. Here they blend with* CAMPANULA PERSICIFOLIA, *Bellflower.*

DICENTRA SPECTABILIS
(dy-SEN-tra) ✿ **Bleeding Heart**

One of the most beautiful of spring-flowering plants with pleasant foliage and beautiful heart-shaped blooms on long stems.

Uses: Excellent as a foliage plant throughout the growing season, becomes a fernlike ground cover; good foil with peonies which disguise the dying foliage.

Maintenance: Shelter from strong winds. Propagate by seed or by division—best done in early spring. Root cuttings should be taken during early summer. Tends to die back in more severe climates. Divide every 2-3 years.

Light: Prefers some shade in hot areas.

Size: 8" - 36" (20 cm - 90 cm) high, 12" - 24" (30 cm - 60 cm) wide.

Color: From white to deep rose pink, heart-shaped blooms on long stems above a mass of delicate bright green foliage.

Blooms: Early spring to summer.

Soil: Well-drained soil with plenty of humus.

Watering: Keep moist but don't let it get soggy.

Origin: North America.

DICTAMNUS ALBUS
(dik-TAME-nus) ✿ **Gas Plant**

The name comes from the fact that a lighted match placed under the flower cluster near the stem will cause a flash as gas ignites. This is reputed

(Zone 6) PAEONIA, *Peony and* DICENTRA EXIMIA ALBA, *White Bleeding Heart combine perfectly with Artemisia 'Silver King'.*

to be the burning bush of the Bible.

Uses: A really attractive plant to put in the middle of a border; very easy care; goes well with lilies and irises.

Maintenance: Keep deadheading during the season. Cut stems back to ground level in fall. Propagate by seed in spring or late summer. Hates being transplanted. Leaves and seed pods are poisonous and can cause dermatitis.

Light: Full sun to light shade.

Size: 24" - 36" (60 cm - 180 cm) high, 30" (75 cm) wide.

Color: Lustrous, dark green leaves above which rise long spikes of wide open long staminate white flowers. Also rose-purple variety.

Blooms: June to July.

Soil: Ordinary even sandy soil, but does best in a good fertile slightly alkaline soil.

Watering: If soil is good it is tolerant of dry conditions.

Origin: Southern Europe to China.

Dropwort *see* FILIPENDULA VULGARIS

ERIGERON SPECIOSUS (e-RIJ-er-on) ❧ **Fleabane**

A member of the Aster family, this is a showy warm summer mass of daisylike flowers.

Uses: Taller varieties make excellent cut flowers. Smaller ones do well in rock gardens; good dried flower.

Maintenance: Tall varieties will need support after rains to prevent them from falling about. Deadhead regularly. Cut stems to ground level in fall. Propagate by division in spring every 3 years.

Light: Full sun to partial shade.

Size: 12" - 24" (30 cm - 60 cm) high, 12" - 24" (30 cm - 60 cm) wide.

Color: Pale lilac, with yellow center, ranging to clear pink, deep pink and purple.

Blooms: June to August.

Soil: Well-drained, not too rich.

Watering: Ordinary care.

Origin: North America and some species in Asia.

Everlasting Sweet Pea *see* LATHYRUS LATIFOLIUS

False Dragonhead *see* PHYSOSTEGIA VIRGINIANA

False Indigo *see* BAPTISIA AUSTRALIS

FILIPENDULA VULGARIS (fil-i-PEN-dew-la) ❧ **Dropwort,**

Meadowsweet, Queen-of-the-Prairie
A charming wild flower of the rose family for gardens with lots of space.

Uses: Good cutting flower. Excellent beside pools and streams and for the back of the border. F. VULGARIS is the best ornamental and combines well with spring bulbs. F. RUBRA will create a truly large stand if you allow it; a magnificent space filler.

Maintenance: Support with stakes. Cut it down to the ground in the fall and if you live in a cold area use a thick winter mulch. Propagate by division in spring. Watch for mildew in dry soils.

Light: Full sun to partial shade.
Size: 12" - 60" (30 cm - 180 cm) high, 12" - 18" (30 cm - 45 cm) wide.
Color: Creamy white to pale and deep pink blooms, on strong, leafy stems.
Blooms: June to July.
Soil: Most prefer damp even wet soils. F. VULGARIS prefers dry, well-drained, limy soils.
Watering: Evenly moist.
Origin: North America, Europe, Asia.

Fleabane *see* ERIGERON SPECIOSUS

Gas Plant *see* DICTAMNUS ALBUS

Gayfeather *see* LIATRIS SPICATA

Ghost Plant *see* ARTEMISIA

Glory-of-the-Snow *see* CHIONODOXA LUCILLAE

Goatsbeard *see* ARUNCUS SYLVESTER

Golden Marguerite *see* ANTHEMIS TINCTORIA KELWAYI

Goldenrod *see* SOLIDAGO

Gooseneck Loosestrife *see* LYSIMACHIA CLETHROIDES

GYPSOPHILA PANICULATA (jip-SOFF-ill-a) **Baby's-breath**
An airy cloud of bloom with a fine feathery texture that provides an ethereal contrast to more substantial perennials.

Uses: Good filler in perennial border. Combines nicely with dianthus hiding its straggly summer foliage. Wonderful as both cut and dried flower. G. REPENS is a splendid ground cover and filler as well.

Maintenance: Large sprays of flowers tend to get top heavy and need staking. Plant in spring or fall. Cut to ground level in fall (late spring in cold areas). Propagate by taking cuttings from the base (basal cuttings) in late spring; stem cuttings in summer: seeds in spring.

Light: Full sun.
Size: 18" - 48" (45 cm - 120 cm) high, 48" (120 cm) wide.
Color: Clouds of tiny white or pink flowers on slender, wiry, branched stems. Small grey-green leaves.
Blooms: June to August.
Soil: Free draining, alkaline soils.
Watering: Do not let dry out, blooms shrivel easily.
Origin: Europe and Northern Asia.

Heartleaf Bergenia *see* BERGENIA CORDIFOLIA

HELENIUM AUTUMNALE (hel-EE-nium) **Sneezeweed**
A robust, bold-flowered, daisylike perennial that's a joy in late summer and early fall borders.

Uses: Good in cutting garden, wild gardens, or meadows—it has a very long season. Use it with chrysanthemums or surround it with cosmos.

Maintenance: Taller varieties need staking. Propagate by division in spring while still dormant. Cut to ground level in fall. Pinching in late spring promotes bushiness and reduces height.

Light: Full sun.
Size: 24" - 60" (60 cm - 150 cm) high, 18" (45 cm) wide.
Color: Yellow with prominent, satiny brown centers. Colors of other varieties range to deeper golds: H. HOOPESII is an orange-yellow and H. A. 'Crimson Beauty' is a carmine.
Blooms: August to September.
Soil: Tolerant of damp soils. Native to swamps and wet meadows in Canada.
Watering: Keep moist.
Origin: North America.

HELLEBORUS FOETIDUS (hell-e-BOR-us) **Stinking Hellebore**
A handsome evergreen perennial with early spring flowers. The name misguides—the smell is really innocuous. There are several of these to consider. H. NIGER, Christmas Rose (see following entry) and H. ORIENTALIS, Lenten Rose.

Uses: Excellent border plant or for edging along a walkway; wonderful winter color.

Maintenance: Deadhead after flowering; don't disturb it if at all possible; all parts are very poisonous; propagate by division after blooming; it self-seeds quite nicely.

Light: Partial sun to full shade.
Size: 18" (45 cm) high, 18" (45 cm) wide.
Color: Rich dark green leaves with flowers of wide open bells in pale greenish yellow tipped with purple.
Blooms: Early to midspring.
Soil: Deep rich neutral or alkaline soil.
Watering: Keep partially moist.
Origin: Europe.

HELLEBORUS NIGER ⁊ Christmas Rose

One of the finest of all garden species with its late blooms.

Uses: Good both in the border and as a cut flower.

Maintenance: A temperamental plant worth all the trouble; top dress with limestone chips to sweeten soil and improve surface drainage, cover crowns in winter; poisonous, if leaves and roots are touched may cause dermatitis; must be propagated vegetatively by division in August or September.

Light: Partial shade but it does need the winter sun.

Size: 8" - 12" (20 cm - 30 cm) high, 18" (45 cm) wide.

Color: Dark evergreen foliage with cup-shaped white flowers 1 to 3 per stem.

Blooms: Late fall, early winter in milder areas.

Soil: Grows in most garden soils; prefers moist ones.

Watering: Keep well-watered.

Origin: Europe.

HEMEROCALLIS (hem-er-o-KAL-is) ⁊ Daylily

From the Greek words *hemera* meaning "day" and *kallos,* meaning "beautiful". All parts of this gorgeous plant are edible from the root (used in Chinese cookery) to the flowers which last for one day but keep coming on in waves. This useful plant manages to be both cheerful and elegant.

Uses: Popular in either formal or informal gardens and as a cut flower; use it as a hedge or along pathways; mass with a succession of colors for a dramatic border on its own. This is a superb plant to collect.

Maintenance: Deadhead daily for neatness. Pull out dried stalks. Leave clumps undisturbed until they become overcrowded then divide the fleshy rhizomes during cool seasons. Just fork them up and pull apart then replant.

Light: Full sun to partial shade.

Size: 15" - 48" (40 cm - 120 cm) high, 24" (60 cm) wide.

Color: Two most common are the H. HYBRIDA that range from cream-white to pinks, oranges, reds, burgundy and mahogany, and the H. FLAVA or yellow daylily.

H. STELLA D'ORO is an excellent variety that blooms continuously. This very tidy plant isn't too large.

All have strong, straplike arching green leaves. Some have a lovely scent.

Blooms: June to August usually for 2 to 3 weeks but with careful choosing you can get extended bloom.

Soil: Tolerant of a wide range of well-drained soils but does best in deep, fertile loam.

Watering: Thorough watering every week during hot weather ensures more abundant blooms.

Origin: Asia.

HEUCHERA SANGUINEA (hew-KER-a) ⁊ Coralbells

This is one of the most reliable of plants. The foliage will stay evergreen except where winters are most severe.

Uses: Good as ground cover; smaller varieties look perfect trailing over paving stones; excellent for cut flowers and foliage interest in the border.

Maintenance: Keep deadheaded. Apply light mulch in cold areas to prevent frost-heave. Divide every 4 to 5 years. Propagate by division in dormant season; by seed in spring, or by cuttings in midsummer.

Light: Full sun to partial shade.

Size: 12" - 18" (30 cm - 45 cm) high, 12" (30 cm) wide.

Color: Dark green or bronze leaves with tiny white, red to pink flowers on long stalks.

H. X BRIZOIDES hybrids come in colors ranging from white to deep scarlet.

Blooms: June to August.

Soil: Ordinary well-drained soil will do, but add organic material —humus, compost.

Watering: Roots are shallow so water well in dry weather.

Origin: North America.

HOSTA SIEBOLDIANA (HOS-ta) ⁊ Plantain Lily

A favorite foliage and shade plant possessed of such variety that it fits into any color scheme. It will survive almost any form of plant abuse.

Uses: Effective ground cover; bank them around trees—they're one of the few plants that can put up with the competition; mass them in a woodland or shade garden; use one of the larger types (H. s. 'Elegans') to anchor a border. It has an almost tropical lushness. A grace note in front of shrubs or in shady courtyards beside water anywhere. One of my ambitions is to have a complete hosta bed with as many varieties as I can find.

(Zone 5) Jeanne Marler's border containing HEMEROCALLIS of every hue proves that broad swathes of one species massed together can be extraordinarily dramatic. There is something in flower throughout most of three seasons.

(Zone 8) Peggy Tupper has a splendid rock garden wall at the back of her house.
SAPONARIA OCYMOIDES, *Rock Soapwort and* GERANIUM SANGUINEUM, *Bloody Cranesbill are*
the most obvious ones in bloom. Behind: ARMERIA, *Thrift;* IBERIS SEMPERVIRENS *coming into bloom;*
English Ivy; TRILLIUM.

Maintenance: A truly low maintenance family of plants. Propagate by division in early spring if you want more of these glorious plants. Take a chunk from the back so you don't mar the beauty of the shape. Be careful of slugs in spring, they can damage new leaves before they unfold; put peat around the edges to keep mud from splattering all over the leaves when it rains.

Light: Partial to full shade.

Size: 6" - 24" (10 cm - 60 cm) high, 12" - 48" (30 cm - 120 cm) wide.

Color: Deep to light greens, yellow-greens and blues in foliage that also has distinctive textures: puckered, smooth, lustrous or glaucous. Some foliage is also variegated with creamy white striping or edging. Flowers are almost secondary but beautiful with waxy blooms of white, lavender or violet. Some are delicately scented. A couple of favorites: H. TOKUDAMA is a blue-green; H. S. 'Francis Williams' has variegated gold and green foliage.

Blooms: July to August.

Soil: Humusy well-drained soil that's shaded and moisture-retentive. Improve soil with leaf mould.

Watering: Do not allow to dry out—they will wilt but recover after watering.

Origin: Asia (Eastern Asia).

IRIS (EYE-ris)
Iris was the messenger of the Greek Gods and these namesakes are almost as ancient. There are so many kinds that it's worthwhile studying them to find the ones that appeal to you most. If you get obsessed there are Iris Societies all over North America.

Uses: Excellent cut flower; stunning effect when massed.

Maintenance: Propagate by dividing rhizomes and replanting (only younger outer sections) right after flowering. Divide every 3-4 years by chopping with a sharp shovel or large knife. Replant the rhizome so the top half shows. Remove winter debris in spring and fertilize—this is when they have their big growth spurt. Remove flower stalks after flowering. Cut back leaves in fall to near ground. In colder areas mulch in winter with straw or twigs.

Light: Full sun to partial shade.

Size: 6" - 36" (15 cm - 90 cm) high, 12" - 36" (30 cm - 90 cm) wide.

Color: All colors from white to a glamorous almost-black with creams through various yellows to near brown pinks and blues. Beautifully scented. Flowers on strong stems above spears of foliage. I. PALLIDA 'Variegata' is worth it for the lovely variegated foliage alone. I. CRISTATA is a native. I. X GERMANICA is the tall bearded variety. I. KAEMPFERI, Japanese Iris, needs lots of water. I. PSEUDACORUS, the Yellow Flag is right for wet areas. I. SIBIRICA is beardless.

Blooms: May to June.

Soil: Depending on the kind—sea-level swamps to Alpine meadows; bearded varieties require free-draining soils. Needs reasonably fertile soil, but not a lot of fertilizer; some will do just fine in thin chalky soils.

Watering: Varies with species.

Origin: North America, Europe, Asia.

Jacob's Ladder *see* POLEMONIUM CAERULEUM

Lady's-mantle *see* ALCHEMILLA MOLLIS

LAMIUM MACULATUM (LAY-mium) ❧ **Spotted Dead Nettle**

A traditional carpeting plant in old-fashioned English gardens. It creeps freely between flagstones, shrubs. Has silver striped leaves that add a bit of brightness to a shaded area.

Uses: Good ground cover for shade; might become a weedlike pest if not controlled.

Maintenance: Adapts to almost any place and can be invasive. After flowering clip plants back to maintain a dense cover of leaves. Propagate by division in spring or fall.

Light: Shade to partial shade.

Size: 12" - 24" (30 cm - 60 cm) high, 12" (30 cm) wide.

Color: Blooms may be white, pink or purple. Foliage is soft green leaves with a central silver stripe; some variegated forms have bright silver splotches on them. Tubular-hooded flowers.

Blooms: May to August.

Soil: Tolerates any type of reasonably well-drained soil. One of the few plants that accepts dry shade.

Watering: Will tolerate dry soil.

Origin: Europe.

Larkspur *see* DELPHINIUM ELATUM

LATHYRUS LATIFOLIUS (LATH-i-rus) ❧ **Everlasting Sweet Pea**

A perennial herb of the pea family, this climber looks just like sweet peas.

Uses: Good on trellises as a privacy screen; attractive on fences behind such plants as lythrum or other tall plants; will ramp among other plants if you let it.

Maintenance: Deadhead all through the season and it'll just keep on blooming; I've tried propagating it without any luck so buy more plants if you need them or plant seeds in the spot where you want them to grow.

Light: Full sun.

Size: Climbs to 9' (2.7 m) high.

Color: Rose, white and lavender blooms; several grow on a single stalk.

Blooms: June to September.

Soil: Deep, well-manured soil.

Watering: Likes lots of water.

Origin: North America, Japan.

Lily *see* LILIUM

LIATRIS SPICATA (ly-AY-tris) ❧ **Gayfeather, Blazing Star**

Originally a star of the Canadian prairies, this is a most agreeable wild flower with terrific foliage.

Uses: Perfect for the wild or meadow garden; in borders gives height without overshadowing the plants around it. It's a good cut flower and will dry well.

Maintenance: Plants die right back in winter so mark their places in fall; propagate by spring-sown seeds or division every 3 to 4 years in spring.

Light: Full sun.

Size: 24" - 72" (60 cm - 180 cm) high, 18" (45 cm) wide.

Color: Unbranched, leafy stems rise to a long-lasting spike of small flower heads in shades of reddish purple that open from the top down.

Blooms: August to September.

Soil: Tolerant of poor soil but prefers moderately fertile, sandy soils, well-drained; add humus.

Watering: Water during dry spells; tolerates some drought but will also grow in excess moisture during the growing season; dislikes winter wet.

Origin: North America.

LILIUM (li-li-um) ❧ **Lily**

This is an enormous family; one that is a pleasure to study and collect. I wouldn't be without several varieties in my garden.

Uses: Make a real statement with dozens of this dramatic plant—all through the border, small ones in the middle, huge ones up against fences.

They are ideal in containers for patio or balcony plants (protected from wind).

Maintenance: Many of the big ones will need staking. They die back. The foliage must be allowed to turn brown (next year's food) so it's best to interplant them with something that's going to disguise the mess; most should be planted about three times the depth of the bulb except L. CANDIDUM which likes shallow planting; mulch to keep the bulbs cool and moist all season; deadhead as soon as the bloom is off—but only to the end of the seedhead—let the rest of the stalk ripen.

Light: Full sun.

Size: From 2' (60 cm) to 9' (270 cm) high.

Color: Runs the gamut from a deep orange to my favorite L. BLACK DRAGON which is a purply black on the outside and a pinky white inside; yellow, pink, red, white.

Blooms: Some start in June and if you plant judiciously you will have blooms in succession until September. L. MARTAGON the Turk's-cap lily is red spotted with black and quite startling. L. REGALE demands as large a swath as you have room for; it's white with a yellow center. L. LONGIFLORUM, the trumpet lily, with many varieties.

Soil: Well-drained, slightly moist.

Watering: Keep moist and water by hand.

Origin: North America, Asia.

LIMONIUM LATIFOLIUM (ly-MO-nium), ❧ **Sea Lavender, Statice**

I love this plant; it's a great substitute for GYPSOPHILA which I don't seem to be able to grow.

Uses: Excellent as dried or fresh cut flowers; in raised beds; use the dwarf forms in the rock garden; if you leave the flowers on their stems, they work well in dried arrangements.

Maintenance: Cut remaining flower stems back to ground in fall. Resents root disturbance. Grows well along sea coasts or near salt marshes. Propagate by seed, under glass in spring.

Light: Full sun.

Size: 24" (60 cm) high, 18" (45 cm) wide.

Color: White or lavender-blue.

Blooms: August to September.

Soil: Prefers well-drained soil with good loam. Will tolerate salt spray.

Watering: Drought resistant.

Origin: Central Europe and Southern Russia.

Lungwort *see* PULMONARIA ANGUSTIFOLIA

LYCHNIS CORONARIA (LIK-nis) ❧ **Rose Campion**

While hard to harmonize in the border, this bright perennial is effective

(Zone 7) LILIUM PYRENAICUM

as a massed planting and the silvery grey foliage is gorgeous.

Uses: Combine this with other grey foliage plants such as EUPHORBIA, DIANTHUS or VERONICA INCANA. The campion is so brilliant it needs some white nearby to tone it down a bit; makes a good specimen. It will naturalize. If you hate the strength of the blooms keep them as foliage plants.

Maintenance: Deadhead unless seeds are wanted. Cut back to ground in fall. The plants are short-lived but they reseed with such profligacy you don't have to worry about losing them; just keep track of the babies and make sure they are in a spot where you want them.

Light: Full sun.

Size: 18" - 30" (45 cm - 70 cm) high, 18" (45 cm) wide.

Color: Suede-soft, silvery grey leaves with magenta flowers.

Blooms: July to August.

Soil: Tolerates dry, poor soils.

Watering: Regular.

Origin: Europe and Asia.

LYSIMACHIA CLETHROIDES (Ly-sim-AK-ia) ❧ **Gooseneck Loosestrife**

If there is the phenomenon of a plant exuding a sense of humor, this is the one. It seems to stretch in the wind on a long gooselike neck in a most elegant manner.

Uses: A marvellous foil to other plants in the middle of the border, gives shape to a drift, combines well with almost any medium-sized plant.

Maintenance: An easy-to-care-for plant that might become invasive so keep an eye on it and keep the clump trimmed in spring. Doesn't mind being divided almost any time.

Light: Sun or shade for part of the day.

Size: 3' (90 cm) high, 2' (60 cm) wide.

Color: White star-shaped flowers.

Blooms: July and August.

Soil: Best in damp soils, or by waterways.

Watering: Keep moist.

Origin: Asia.

LYTHRUM SALICARIA (LY-thrum) ❧ **Purple Loosestrife**

This flashy plant is viewed as dangerous in really boggy country where it will naturalize all too readily. There are, however, lots of less invasive cultivars that do a splendid job in ordinary borders as well as wet areas.

Uses: In marshes; wet meadows. Excellent beside ponds and streams. A good focal point in a border. I like it surrounded by ARTEMISIA, LAVATERA, VERONICA INCANA; ROSA RUBRIFOLIA and ACHILLEA FILIPENDULA 'Moonshine'.

Maintenance: Control it in boggy situations by keeping trimmed; isolate plants for specimens; if you have huge areas to cover, this is your plant. Long blooming if deadheaded back to the next stem. Propagate by dividing roots in fall or spring.

Light: Full sun to partial shade.

Size: 24" - 72" (60 cm - 180 cm) high, 24" (60 cm) wide.

Color: Red-purple to pink blooms on spikes. Foliage turns an attractive bronzy shade in fall.

Blooms: July to September.

Soil: Prefers wet, marshy, but grows well in garden soil too.

Watering: Keep moist.

Origin: Europe (naturalized in North America).

Maiden Pink *see* DIANTHUS DELTOIDES

Meadowsweet *see* FILIPENDULA VULGARIS

Michaelmas Daisy *see* ASTER NOVI-BELGII

Monkshood *see* ACONITUM NAPELLUS

Moss Pink *see* PHLOX SUBULATA

NEPETA (NEP-et-a) ❧ **Catmint**

A must for traditional gardens with its aromatic grey-green leaves. Don't confuse this with catnip—that's N. CATARIA which should be used as a pot plant unless you want every cat in the neighborhood rolling around in the border.

Uses: Beautifully aromatic (sold as MUSSINII in nurseries). This is a perfect foil for more dramatically colored plants; quite happy on a sea coast; use in foreground of old-fashioned roses; combined with stachys makes a dramatic edging along a path or sidewalk.

Maintenance: After blooming cut back by half to encourage second bloom. This is a hybrid so seeds are sterile. Propagate by division or stem cuttings in spring; doesn't much like humidity.

Light: Full sun.

Size: 9" - 12" (22 cm - 30 cm) high, 18" (45 cm) wide.

Color: Lavender with beautifully subtle grey-green foliage.

Blooms: July to September.

Soil: Well-drained, ordinary soil.

Watering: Tolerates drought.

Origin: Europe and Asia.

Obedient Plant *see* PHYSOSTEGIA VIRGINIANA

Oriental Poppy *see* PAPAVER ORIENTALE

PAEONIA LACTIFLORA (pee-O-nia) ❧ **Peony**

Right out of an 18th century still life. Apart from its great beauty it is dependable, long-lived, very hardy and requires little maintenance. A perfect plant.

Uses: Excellent as cut flowers. Ideal for planting between shrubs, or as an anchor at either end of a border. I almost like it best for the foliage which is attractive all season and turns a sensual bronze in fall. Use it to cover up the muck left behind by most bulbs.

Maintenance: Enrich with manure but avoid the roots; might need staking; plant in fall with crowns no more than 1 inch (2.5 centimeters) below soil level. Light shade in extremely hot locations but keep away from overhanging trees; normally they don't like being disturbed but I've moved a couple when they were young without any drastic consequences. They take a couple of years to grab hold and flower, but don't despair.

Light: Full sun or light shade.

Size: 24" - 48" (60 cm - 120 cm) high, 24" - 48" (60 cm - 120 cm) wide.

Color: Common garden peony has pink, yellow, peach flowers in double or single blooms on reddish brown stems above strong, dark green foliage that turns bronzy in fall. Species peonies are particularly lovely though not quite as showy as the hybrids.

Blooms: May to June but if you select the varieties carefully you can extend the bloom period.

Soil: Grows best in fairly heavy, well-drained soil, acid or alkaline, enriched with organic matter before planting.

Watering: Regular.

Origin: Asia (North Eastern Asia).

PAPAVER ORIENTALE (pap-AY-ver)
❧ **Oriental Poppy, Poppy**

If you want a hit of flamboyance, plant at least three or four of the one hundred varieties.

Uses: Can be used as cut flowers—pick as buds in early morning; burn stem to prevent bleeding. Use in sunny borders in clumps; among grasses or vegetables.

Maintenance: Keep deadheading, leaves will yellow and wither by midsummer so tidy to crown level. To prevent bare spaces in summer, combine with other plants that come into flower later on in the season (asters, LIMONIUM, or annuals such as NIGELLA). Propagate by root cuttings in late summer. Doesn't much like being transplanted, which you should do in fall, but once you have them they are with you forever.

Light: Full sun.

Size: 24" - 48" (60 cm - 120 cm) high, 24" - 36" (60 cm - 90 cm) wide.

Color: White, salmon pink, watermelon to the best-known bright red with deep purple at the base. Petals are beautiful frilly things. Stems and coarse leaves are bristly and rather attractive.

Blooms: Late May to June.

Soil: Well-drained, deep rich soil.

Watering: Not too much water.

Origin: Mediterranean Region and Persia.

PARTHENOCISSUS QUINQUEFOLIA
(par-thee-no-SISS-us) ❧ **Virginia Creeper**

A deciduous native vine with rich red autumn color.

Uses: Needs no support, excellent as a creeper; for crawling up walls, trees (won't strangle them), sides of houses; used for a summer screen.

Maintenance: Provide support for young plants; pinch back to encourage branching; propagate by stem cuttings; prune according to your space requirements; if limited, then cut back to ground in late fall.

Light: Full sun to partial shade.

Size: Can grow up to 25' (7.5 m) a year depending on how favorable the conditions are.

Color: Leaves are dark green, turn scarlet in fall; produces small blue fruit attractive to birds.

Blooms: Turns crimson in autumn.

Soil: Humus-rich, well-drained.

Watering: Keep moist.

Origin: North America.

PENSTEMON BARBATUS
(pen-STEE-mon) ❧ **Beard-tongue**

A native American wild flower that looks a bit like foxglove and has evergreen foliage. One of the most beautiful of the wild flowers.

Uses: Exceptionally hardy in its native Western habitat. Looks good in mixed borders; rock or wall gardens.

Maintenance: These are short-lived plants but worth the trouble. Cut back to crown in fall, protect with cloches in cold areas. Mulch with pea gravel for sharp drainage. Propagate by seed. They can be temperamental outside their natural home in the Pacific Northwest, Rockies and Prairies.

Light: Full sun or light shade.

Size: 12" - 24" (30 cm - 60 cm) high, 12" - 24" (30 cm - 60 cm) wide.

(Zone 9) This seaside border designed by George Radford is in a public park.
In bloom left to right: SAXIFRAGA URBIUM; DIANTHUS X ALLWOODII, *Border Carnation;* POLEMONIUM CAERULEUM, *Jacob's ladder;* GYPSOPHILA REPENS, *Creeping Gypsophila;* HESPERIS MATRONALIS, *Dame's Rocket. The clump of* GERANIUM *is backed by* PAPAVER ORIENTALE, *Oriental Poppy, and* LUPINUS, *lupine.*

Color: Flower sprays range from pink to purple. Foliage is evergreen.

Blooms: July and August.

Soil: Good drainage a must; ordinary soil that has sand and gravel in it is appreciated by these plants.

Watering: Keep well watered.

Origin: North America.

Peony SEE PAEONIA LACTIFLORA

PHLOX PANICULATA (flox) ❧ **Phlox**

This most traditional of all starter-plants is a native North American.

Uses: Superb in borders, rockeries and wild gardens. A good cut flower. Plant in front of a rugosa shrub and behind SANTOLINA CHAMAECYPARIS-SUS, Cotton Lavender, to hide the rather woody stems, in combination with ASTILBE or ACONITUM.

Maintenance: Mildew is a problem with this plant. Move the plant to a spot where there's good air circulation if it persists. Deadheading keeps most of them going for weeks but there are some, you'll have to be observant about this, that bloom a second time on their own. For much stronger plants, divide every three years in fall. Replant only small strong, outer divisions. Nematodes (nasty little worms) can be a problem so check the roots to make sure they are clean. Seeds are not recommended as the colors may come out muddy. Propagate by division in fall or spring, or by root division in dormant season.

Light: Full sun.

Size: 24" - 60" (60 cm - 150 cm) high, 24" (60 cm) wide.

Color: Ranges from pure white through pink to red, lavender and purple often with a contrasting eye. Blooms have a pleasant scent.

Blooms: August to September.

Soil: Rich, well-drained, deep, porous.

Watering: Water deeply at root level in dry spells and try not to get the foliage wet.

Origin: North America.

PHLOX SUBULATA (flox) ❧ **Moss Pink**

A bright green mat with a highly textured surface covered with bright flowers in spring.

Uses: Rock gardens, Alpine gardens. Tumbles nicely over a trough garden, down a rock fall, or in paving pockets. P. SUBULATA is a first-rate ground cover and hanging rock wall plant.

Maintenance: Shear plants after flowering to keep them compact. Propagate by separating clumps after flowering and replanting.

Light: Full sun.

Size: 4" (10 cm) high, 18" (45 cm) wide.

Color: Blossoms vary from white to blue to crimson with intense green foliage.

Blooms: May to June.

Soil: Good, well-drained sandy soil.

Watering: Regular.

Origin: North America.

PHYSOSTEGIA VIRGINIANA (fy-so-STEE-jia) ❧ **Obedient Plant, False Dragonhead, Virginia Lion's Heart**

A truly cheerful flower. It showed up in my garden as a surprise many

(Zone 5) Bridget Hutchison planted this well balanced group: PHLOX PANICULATA, *Border Phlox;* DIGITALIS, *Foxglove; in front of the stand of* COSMOS *is a white* GERANIUM.

years ago and I've loved it ever since. The hinged stalks keep whatever position they are pushed in; therefore, the nickname Obedient.

Uses: A good cut flower for both the border and the wild garden.

Maintenance: This plant is extremely easy to grow and blooms for a long time. But it does spread rapidly and needs division every 2 to 3 years. Apply mulch. Cut down in late autumn. Propagate by replanting outer portions of plant in fall or spring.

Light: Full sun, partial shade.

Size: 36" (90 cm) high, 18" (45 cm) wide.

Color: Dense terminal cluster of white or pink flowers.

Blooms: July and August.

Soil: Moisture-retentive, slightly acid soil.

Watering: Water freely in dry spells.

Origin: North America.

Pincushion Flower *see* SCABIOSA CAUCASICA

Pinks *see* DIANTHUS DELTOIDES

Plantain Lily *see* HOSTA SIEBOLDIANA

POLEMONIUM CAERULEUM (po-lee-MO-nium) **Jacob's Ladder**

A late spring plant with blue flowers over delicate foliage still appealing after flowers are finished for the season.

Uses: Front of perennial borders in shadier areas of the garden.

Maintenance: Remove flower stems close to the foliage after blooming. Propagate by division in fall or spring but be careful not to damage the brittle stems if you decide to divide in spring. It self-seeds freely. Pluck out the seedlings and place them where wanted in spring or fall.

Light: Partial shade to shade. Full sun in areas where summers are moderate.

Size: 12" - 36" (30 cm - 90 cm) high, 24" (60 cm) wide.

Color: Leaflets arranged like rungs of a ladder—good as simple foliage plants once blooming is over. The loose clustered flowers are usually blue.

Blooms: June to July.

Soil: Ordinary soil enriched with humus.

Watering: Moist conditions are best.

Origin: Europe and Asia.

POLYGONATUM ODORATUM (po-lig-o-NA-tum) **Solomon's-seal**

Member of the lily family, this wild flower grows from fleshy roots. Name derives from rounded seal-like scars on the upper surfaces of the rhizomes and from its supposed ability to seal wounds. One of the most elegant of all woodland plants.

Uses: The backbone of a wild or woodland garden. It combines well with rhododendrons and hostas and is the perfect companion to early spring bulbs and ferns.

Maintenance: Little care is generally required. Mulch in spring to conserve moisture. Cut back to ground in fall. Propagate by division in fall or spring.

Light: Partial shade to full shade.

Size: 24" - 48" (60 cm - 120 cm) high, 24" (60 cm) wide.

Color: The graceful arching stems have pairs of upward-curving leaves with creamy white bell flowers topped with green.

Blooms: June.

Soil: Ordinary, fertile soil of woodland type.

Watering: Prefers moist soil but is drought resistant.

Origin: North America.

Poppy *see* PAPAVER ORIENTALE

Primrose *see* PRIMULA AURICULA

PRIMULA AURICULA (PRIM-u-la) **Primrose**

Among the primroses are some of our most familiar and enchanting spring flowers. There are thirty different sections in this genus. You can become a collector.

Uses: In Europe and favorable North American climates, it's used as a bedding plant. It combines well with all the other shade-loving plants. Mixes nicely with violets to make a pretty spring ground cover. Used widely in wild or country gardens beneath large trees on the lawn. Mass for a dramatic impact in spring.

Maintenance: Mulch lightly to avoid winter heaving. Divide after blooming in spring or propagate by seed in late spring or early summer as soon as they ripen.

Light: Partial shade.

Size: 6" (15 cm) high, 9" (20 cm) wide.

Color: Predominantly yellow but colors range to red, purple, pink and white.

Blooms: Early spring. P. AURICULA and P. DENTICULATA are the hardiest.

Soil: Fertile soil with plenty of humus.

Watering: Plenty of water especially during dry spells. Does not do well in areas of summer drought.

Origin: Europe and Asia.

PULMONARIA ANGUSTIFOLIA (pul-mo-NAY-ria) **Lungwort**

This cheery plant has blue flowers opening from pink buds. The silver-dipped foliage is evergreen in mild areas. It is a great starter plant that's almost impossible to destroy.

(Zone 8) Van Dusen Gardens has a fine stand of PRIMULA CAPITATA.

Purple Loosestrife *see* LYTHRUM SALICARIA

Queen-of-the-Prairie *see* FILIPENDULA VULGARIS

Rose Campion *see* LYNCHNIS CORONARIA

Sage Brush *see* ARTEMISIA

SAPONARIA OCYMOIDES
(sap-o-NAY-ria) ❧ Soapwort
Closely related to pinks and carnations. Called SAPONARIA because bruised leaves or stems of some varieties have been used in soap making.
Uses: Use in combination with pinks and carnations. Pretty as a trailer over rocks and walls, and in rock gardens; not as effective in the border.
Maintenance: Shear hard after blooming for neatness and to encourage vegetative growth. Propagate by cuttings in summer or early fall, and by seed in spring.
Light: Full sun.
Size: 3" (8 cm) high, 24" (60 cm) wide.
Color: A cushion of pale green leaves is almost hidden by a mass of bright, rose pink blooms arranged in showy clusters.
Blooms: June to August.
Soil: Will grow in almost any soil.
Watering: Regular.
Origin: Europe.

SCABIOSA CAUCASICA
(skab-i-O-sa) ❧ **Pincushion Flower**
Charming old-fashioned plant with wonderful blowzy blossoms.
Uses: An almost perfect flower for cutting. Use it as a back-up for other old-fashioned flowers such as dianthus or pinks in the garden, and you'll have a soft romantic display most of the summer.

Uses: Good ground cover in semi-shaded places. Does best under deciduous trees. Another good plant for covering up the detritus of spring bulbs.
Maintenance: Spread mulch beneath leaf mounds in late spring—use either peat or rotted manure. Propagate by division of creeping rootstock in fall.
Light: Partial shade to shade.

Size: 9" - 24" (25 cm - 60 cm) high, 18" - 24" (45 cm - 60 cm) wide.
Color: Long, hairy oval leaves are green splashed with silver. Flowers start pink and mature to blue.
Blooms: April to June.
Soil: Prefers moisture-retentive soil.
Watering: Keep moist.
Origin: Europe.

Maintenance: Deadhead regularly. Cut stems back to ground in fall. Propagate by division every 3 to 4 years. This helps encourage prolific flowering in spring. Sow seeds in spring; however, they may not grow true to type.

Light: Full sun.

Size: 12" - 24" (30 cm - 60 cm) high, 12" - 24" (30 cm - 60 cm) wide.

Color: Clear blue flowers.

Blooms: June to September.

Soil: Good garden soil on the limy side.

Watering: Keep moist in summer, well drained in winter.

Origin: Europe, Asia and Africa.

Sea Lavender *see* LIMONIUM LATIFOLIUM

SEDUM SPECTABILIS (SEE-dum)
Stonecrop

An extremely large genus of alpine plants some of which will sit on rocks and walls. Get as many as you have room for in your garden. They are among the very best beginner plants. s. s. 'Autumn Joy' has three seasons—all delightful.

Uses: Ideal for rockeries, trough or alpine gardens, on walls and even on roofs. Some of the more dwarf forms can be used for edging.

Maintenance: These incredibly forgiving plants need a minimum of attention. Propagate most of them by taking off a chunk and sticking it back into the earth.

Light: Full sun to partial shade.

Size: 6" - 18" (15 cm - 45 cm) high, 12" - 24" (30 cm - 60 cm) wide.

Color: Small fleshy leaves with clustered, starry little flowers in white, yellow, pink and red.

Blooms: August to September.

Soil: Grows easily in lean, fast-draining soil.

Watering: Water sparingly.

Origin: North America, Europe and Asia.

Serbian Bellflower *see* CAMPANULA POSCHARSKYANA

Sneezeweed *see* HELENIUM AUTUMNALE

Snow-in-summer *see* CERASTIUM TOMENTOSUM

Soapwort see SAPONARIA OCYIMOIDES

SOLIDAGO (sol-i-DAY-go)
Goldenrod

Often seen in late summer as great swaths of gold along railway embankments or in abandoned fields. This poor plant is blamed for hay fever but it's a bum rap—the seedheads are too heavy to drift on the air. People confuse it with ragweed. An important part of late summer, wildflower display.

Uses: Combines nicely with asters (Michaelmas Daisy) in wild gardens. Good as a cut flower. s. GOLDENMOSA is the hybrid best for the garden forming regular clumps.

Maintenance: Staking necessary in

(Zone 3) This tailored border and fence designed by Jon Lowry complement each other: Left to right: LUPINUS, *Lupine;* RANUNCULUS, *Buttercup; Marguerites; and a collection of beautiful* AQUILEGIA, *Columbine.*

windy sites. Cut to ground level in fall. Can be invasive, so regular division is a must. This is a very hardy plant.

Light: Full sun to light shade.

Size: 30" - 36" (75 cm - 90 cm) high.

Color: Foliage is yellow-green with mimosa-colored sprays of yellow flowers.

Blooms: Late August to September.

Soil: Thrives in soils of average fertility.

Watering: Normal.

Origin: North America.

Solomon's-seal *see* POLYGONATUM ODORATUM

Speedwell *see* VERONICA INCANA

Spotted Dead Nettle *see* LAMIUM MACULATUM

Statice *see* LIMONIUM LATIFOLIUM

Stinking Hellebore *see* HELLEBORUS FOETIDUS

Stonecrop *see* SEDUM SPECTABILIS

Thyme *see* THYMUS VULGARIS

THYMUS VULGARIS (TI-mus)
❧ **Thyme**
Low aromatic creepers belonging to the mint family. There are dozens of them and I like all of them.

Uses: Terrific ground cover with a pleasant scent when touched or walked on. They can't take a lot of traffic. Good as low edging. Given the extraordinary variety, this is a good genus to collect.

Maintenance: Shear back flowers and keep chopping away at the edges to keep a nice shape. Prune out winter damage. Propagate by division of plants by taking out clumps in spring.

Light: Prefers full sun.

Size: 6" - 12" (15 cm - 30 cm) high, 24" (60 cm) wide.

Color: White to pink to purple. Essentially evergreen with whirls of asymmetric flowers. T. VULGARIS is attractive to bees. T. PSEUDOLANUGINOSUS, Woolly Thyme, has beautiful grey foliage and looks lovely between terrace stones.

T. MONTANUS RUBRA, T. M. ALBA, both have interesting texture and delicate flowers.

Blooms: July to August.

Soil: Prefers light, free-draining soils of moderate fertility.

Watering: Tolerates dry conditions.

Origin: Europe with some varieties in Western Asia and North Africa.

(Zone 5) Amy Stewart's garden has many Thymes including on the right, THYMUS X SERPYLLUM, *Mother-of-Thyme.*

TRILLIUM GRANDIFLORUM (TRILL-ium) ❧ **Wake-robin**

A genus of the lily family. An exquisite plant that has all its parts in groups of three, thus the name. Never pick this plant in the wild. Buy only from nurseries that guarantee it's been cultivated.

Uses: Good in a woodland garden or a semi-shaded courtyard.

Maintenance: Left alone, it will gradually increase. The leaves disappear when the plant goes dormant in summer, so mark the site. Place trilliums where they won't have to compete with a lot of surface roots but near larger plants that will cover up the hollow space they inevitably leave. Rhizomes are propagated by division in dormant season. Set 3-4 inches (8-10 centimeters) deep.

Light: Partial shade.

Size: 12" - 15" (30 cm - 40 cm) high, 12" (30 cm) wide.

Color: Clumps of dark green foliage with exquisite white flowers. There are also strains of deep purple flowers.

Blooms: April to June.

Soil: Moist, humus-rich soil.

Watering: Never allow to dry out.

Origin: North America.

VERONICA INCANA (ver-ON-i-ca) ❧ **Speedwell**

There are many kinds of VERONICA and I have a soft spot for almost all of them. Especially V. INCANA which has blue flowers and a silvery foliage.

Uses: Perfect foreground plant in border.

Maintenance: Easy to grow. Cut down to ground level in late fall. Propagate by division or basal cuttings in spring every 3 to 4 years.

Light: Full sun to partial shade.

Size: 12" - 24" (30 cm - 60 cm) high, 18" (45 cm) wide.

Color: Low clumps of silvery grey

herbage with spires of clear blue.

Blooms: July to August.

Soil: Average, well-drained soil. Weak and sprawling growth means your soil is too rich.

Watering: Keep moist.

Origin: Europe and Asia.

Virginia Creeper *see* PARTHENOCISSUS QUINQUEFOLIA

Virginia Lion's Heart *see* PHYSOSTEGIA VIRGINIANA

Wake-robin *see* TRILLIUM GRANDIFLORUM

Wall Rock Cress *see* ARABIS CAUCASICA

Wild Columbine *see* AQUILEGIA CANADENSIS

Wormwood *see* ARTEMISIA

Yarrow *see* ACHILLEA

More plants that will grow well in zones 2 and 3:

AJUGA REPTANS, **Bugleweed, ground cover**
ARMERIA MARITIMA, **Thrift, Sea Pink**
BRUNNERA MACROPHYLLA, **Siberian Bugloss**
CONVALLARIA MAJALIS, **Lily of the Valley**
DRYAS OCTOPETALA
ECHINACEA PURPUREA, **Purple Coneflower**
ECHINOPS RITRO, **Globe Thistle**
EPIMEDIUM X RUBRUM, **Bishop's Hat**
ERYSIMUM ASPERUM, **Siberian Wallflower**
EURYOPS ACRAEUS
FOENICULUM VULGARE PURPUREUM, **Bronze Fennel**
GALANTHUS NIVALIS, **Snowdrop**
GENTIANA ACAULIS, **Trumpet Gentian**
HELIANTHUS X MULTIFLORUS, **Sunflower**
IBERIS SEMPERVIRENS, **Everlasting Candytuft**
IPOMOEA TRICOLOR, **Morning Glory**
LYSIMACHIA PUNCTATA OR L. CLETHROIDES, **Loosestrife**
MACLEAYA MICROCARPA, **Plume Poppy**
POLYGONUM AFFINE, **Himalayan Fleece-flower**
RUDBECKIA NITIDA, **Coneflower**
SALIX RETICULATA, **Netleaved Willow**
SCILLA SIBIRICA, **Siberian Squill**
SMILACINA RACEMOSA, **False Solomon's-seal**
THERMOPSIS MONTANA, **Mountain Thermopsis**
TIARELLA CORDIFOLIA, **Foamflower**
VERBASCUM BLATTARIA, **Moth Mullein**
VINCA MINOR, **Periwinkle**
VIOLA CANADENSIS, **Canada Violet**

HARDINESS ZONE FOUR

The range of this zone covers the interior and mountainous regions of British Columbia; north shore of Lake Superior across central Ontario; Quebec along the St. Lawrence River; the interior of New Brunswick; along the Gulf of St. Lawrence; and the interior of Newfoundland. Across the central northern United States and New England. And, of course, pockets that exist in low lying areas of Zone 5.

In these areas winters tend to be cold, and summers to be hot. One striking element in favor of the garden is a reliable snow cover in most areas. This protects plants as a natural mulch. Place snow fences around certain areas that aren't as well shielded.

This zone is warmer than two and three mainly because of higher rainfall. It has a consistent cover of winter snow which means that many plants survive because they are not as vulnerable to disastrous freeze-thaw cycles. Bulbs do phenomenally well in this zone as do an enormous variety of perennials. Longer days compensate to some extent for a slightly shorter growing season than higher zones. Be sure to let foliage on perennials ripen fully. It may look a bit grungy but photosynthesis carries on through the leaves. Keep evergreens watered during dry spells, especially just before the ground freezes. Since evergreens don't become entirely dormant, water keeps transpiring from leaves and needles even in winter. Here are some grasses that you might try in this zone: CALAMAGROSTIS ARUNDINACEA 'Karl Forster', Feather Reed grass, turns pink to purple to gold. In shade, plant CAREX MORROWII 'variegata', variegated Japanese Sedge; and SPARTINA PECTINATA 'aureo-marginata', variegated Prairie Cord Grass, slightly invasive but will stabilize banks of streams or ponds.

CLIMATIC CONSIDERATIONS:
Average annual minimum temperatures:
-30°F to -20°F   -35°C to -29°C
Number of growing days: 195

Indicator shrubs: HYDRANGEA PANICULATA 'Grandiflora', Peegee Hydrangea; PHILADELPHUS 'BOUQUET BLANC', Mock Orange; TAXUS CUSPIDATA, Japanese Yew.

(Zone 8) Kathie Leishman combines CORYDALIS LUTEA *and* GERANIUM SANGUINEUM.

SELECTED LISTINGS
FOR HARDINESS ZONE FOUR

ACTINIDIA KOLOMIKTA
(ak-tin-ID-ia) ❧ **Kiwi Vine**

A vigorous climbing plant that is related to the vine bearing Kiwi fruit, A. CHINENSIS. Fragrant flowers are one of its strong attractions.

Uses: As a screen, to train as an espalier or grow along a wall or fence; if you want fruit buy male and female plants.

Maintenance: South facing walls are ideal and produce a more pronounced variegation. Plant needs training on strong supports when young. Prune to shape in early spring. You have to keep a firm grip on this plant. In warmer climates, it can grow like a demonic presence if you let it.

Light: Full sun.

Size: Climbs 25' (8 m) high.

Color: Male plant has the large pink to white blotch at the end of every leaf; insignificant white flower.

Blooms: Foliage is the chief interest.

Soil: Fertile and humus-rich well-drained soil.

Watering: Keep moist.

Origin: Asia.

ARISAEMA TRIPHYLLUM (a-riss-EEM-ma) ❧ **Jack-in-the-pulpit**

A member of the Arum family, it's one of those mysterious hooded plants that seem to thrive in woodlands (Zones 4 - 9).

Uses: We're used to thinking of woodland plants as spring bloomers but this one comes out much later and is a welcome addition to the woodland garden for that reason. Its value lies not only in the fascinating hooded flower but also the striped foliage and berries which appear in fall.

Maintenance: Be sure to keep the soil cool and well mulched; be careful of slugs.

Light: Partial shade.

Size: 12" (30 cm) high.

Color: Green striped foliage, purple flowers.

Blooms: Summer with fall berries.

Soil: Rich in humus, moisture-retentive.

Watering: Keep moist.

Origin: Asia.

ASTILBE (as-TIL-be) ❧ **Spirea**

Attractive plants with fern foliage somewhat like spirea. Member of the SAXIFRAGA family.

Uses: Some varieties are good as pot plants, others look gorgeous by pools, streams; ideal for a shady garden; the dwarf version makes a first-rate ground cover. If you plant them along a pretty fence they look like a cloud when they're in full bloom.

Maintenance: Protect from mid-day sun. This plant doesn't like very high summer temperatures and does best in temperate climates; in warmer areas mulch with well-aged manure; propagate by division every three years; if you can bear to cut off the spent blooms, they make good dried flowers. Because they look so appealing, I prefer to leave them on through winter and cut them back to the ground in early spring.

Light: Partial shade.

Size: 18" - 48" (45 cm - 120 cm) high, 12" - 30" (30 cm - 75 cm) wide.

Color: Ranges from a white to rosy pink to deep crimson; foliage is ferny and attractive after the bloom is spent and turns almost russet in fall.

A. CHINENSIS 'Pumila' is a tidy ground cover 10 inches (25 centimeters) high in a particularly attractive rosy-mauve shade.

Blooms: June and July.

Soil: Cool moist soil rich in humus.

Watering: Keep fairly moist.

Origin: East Asia.

ASTRANTIA MAJOR
(as-TRAN-shia) ❧ **Masterwort**

This is an easy to cultivate plant that will give you pleasure through three seasons and will grow on almost any site.

Uses: Excellent for cutting. Use along streams and ponds; in a shade garden it's especially welcome.

Maintenance: If you keep dead-heading you'll get flowers right up until fall. Propagate by division in dormant season. Sow seeds in September in trays and place in cold frame. In spring plant in nursery bed; then move to a permanent location the following spring.

Light: Sun to partial shade.

Size: 24" - 36" (60 cm - 90 cm) high, 12" - 18" (30 cm - 45 cm) wide.

Color: Greenish white bracts (these are diminished leaves) flushed with pink or green, tipped with tiny pink or white flowers. There are many cultivars.

Blooms: June to July.

Soil: Ordinary fertile garden soil.

Watering: Keep evenly moist.

Origin: Europe.

BEE BALM *see* **Monarda didyma**

CENTRANTHUS RUBER
(sen-TRAN-thus) ❧ **Jupiter's-beard, Keys-of-Heaven, Valerian**

Noted for its fierce red flowers, this plant is often seen gracing old

(Zone 5) This corner of Amy Stewart's garden features OENOTHERA TETRAGONA, *Evening Primrose in a neat combination with* ALCHEMILLA, ASTILBE, *Lily and Siberian Iris —an absolutely striking arrangement of plants.*

walls and cliff faces around the Mediterranean. It's very hardy.

Uses: Suitable for rock walls where they can be contained; in wild gardens; combine with grey and silver foliage plants and you have the start of a Mediterranean garden.

Maintenance: Seedlings are profligate but the color may vary. It's preferable to divide in spring or plant seeds in the fall. Cut back to ground level in fall.

Light: Full sun to partial shade.

Size: 18" - 36" (45 cm - 90 cm) high, 12" - 24" (30 cm - 60 cm) wide.

Color: Fragrant flowers vary from carmine to rosy pink. Foliage is a bold fleshy, grey-green.

Blooms: June to September.

Soil: Poor chalky soil will keep it from spreading too quickly and give you a more compact plant. Soil should be well drained.

Watering: Drought resistant. Watering prevents woody growth. Dislikes damp shade.

Origin: Europe; Mediterranean area.

CHRYSANTHEMUM X MORIFOLIUM (Kris-ANTH-em-um) **Garden Chrysanthemum**

One of the major reasons to welcome fall is to watch these cheerful plants. They were as popular two thousand years ago as they are today. Every garden, no matter how small, should have room for at least one.

Uses: Filling out the late summer to autumn border. Good in the middle of a border or as a background plant. Wonderful cut flower.

Maintenance: Pinching back is important to this plant no matter what cultivar (and there are dozens) you prefer. Start when they are 6 - 8 inches (15 - 20 centimeters) high and then again when they reach the same height. Keep doing this until the middle of July and then let them go. You'll end up with a fairly bushy plant. After the first frost hits, cut them back to the ground or fold stems into the center to protect the crown and cut down in spring. Divide every three years to keep a good strong flower.

Light: Full sun to very light shade.
Size: 12" - 24" (30 cm - 120 cm) high, 12" (30 cm) wide.
Color: All colors except blue
Blooms: From August to October depending on cultivar.
Soil: Rich, well-drained.
Watering: Water once a week in dry spells; in autumn don't get the foliage wet (mildew); cut back on watering once they're in bloom.
Origin: Orient, Europe and North America.

CHRYSANTHEMUM X SUPERBUM
(kris-ANTH-em-um) ❧ **Shasta Daisy**
A most satisfying starter plant. It has a certain elegance when the plant is young.

Uses: Often used in wild gardens and in meadows. Good as cut flowers. Tolerates coastal conditions but isn't happy with a lot of humidity. Use large forms as anchor plants in a border, dwarf forms as edging plants.

Maintenance: Feed throughout growing season; deadhead to clean up plant and extend blooming time—cut down to the next branch that has stem developing. Pinching back tall cultivars to encourage bushiness will mean smaller blooms. Cut down to about 3 inches (8 centimeters) in fall. Normally propagate by division every third year in spring but I've moved them after blooming without any problem.

Light: Full sun to partial shade.
Size: 12" - 36" (30 cm - 90 cm) high, 18" - 24" (45 cm - 60 cm) wide.
Color: Dark green foliage in bushy clumps. Flowers are white with yellow eyes, resembling the ox-eye daisy only much larger.
Blooms: June to August.
Soil: Rich, well-drained soil.
Watering: Copious watering in dry weather.
Origin: Europe (Pyrenees).

Climbing Hydrangea *see* HYDRANGEA ANOMALA PETIOLARIS

Cranesbill *see* GERANIUM ENDRESSII

DORONICUM CORDATUM
(do-RON-ik-um) ❧ **Leopard's Bane**
This earliest of the daisies to bloom brings an aura of sunlight into the border when most things are in foliage.

Uses: Good for early spring color and as a cut flower. Combines well with spring bulbs such as tulips and narcissi. Plant scilla around it. Put it near a later blooming plant that will cover up the bare spot it will leave when it goes into dormancy—not a good plant for massing.

Maintenance: Apply spring mulch over the shallow roots. Propagate by division in the summer dormant season. Be sure to mark the spot. Tidy plants by removing dead foliage in fall.

Light: Light shade.
Size: 12" - 24" (30 cm - 60 cm) high, 12" - 18" (30 cm - 45 cm) wide.
Color: Bright yellow flowers over bright green heart-shaped foliage.
Blooms: Early spring. Foliage will die back in hot weather—mark the spot or you might pull it up in spring.
Soil: Woodland-type soil with lots of humus.
Watering: Keep moist.
Origin: Sicily to Asia Minor.

False Sunflower *see* HELIOPSIS HELIANTHOIDES

Garden Chrysantheum *see* CHRYSANTHEMUM X MORIFOLIUM

GERANIUM ENDRESSII
(jer-AY-nium) ❧ **Cranesbill**
This is not the pot plant—that's a zonal geranium or PELARGONIUM. These are the true geraniums. The seeds of the cranesbill give it the name. G. ENDRESSII and G. SANGUINEUM are safe from Zone 4; G. ROBERTIANUM, Herb Robert, is safe in Zone 3.

Uses: Excellent as a ground cover in dry conditions. Use in rock gardens and along perennial borders; even good in shade where it won't bloom; however, the foliage is so nice it's a shame not to employ it where you can.

Maintenance: Essentially free of pests and diseases. Keeps on flowering if you deadhead regularly. Shear back after blooming to get second flowering in fall. Leave clumps to spread undisturbed. Propagate by division in dormant season.

Light: Full sun to partial shade in very warm areas.
Size: 12" - 18" (30 cm - 45 cm) high, 24" (60 cm) wide.
Color: Dense layer of pale green foliage; blooms are mainly pink but some cultivars go from white to blue to violet. G. 'Johnson's Blue' is one of

(Zone 9)Susan Ryley has used one of my favorite color combinations: STACHYS *with peonies and*
THALICTRUM; CEANOTHUS *'Gloire de Versailles' in the background.*
Violet blue DELPHINIUM *is wonderful in this stunning border.*

the famous blue geraniums with a long season. G. SANGUINEUM 'Album' is a low plant with white flowers.

Blooms: June to September depending on cultivar.

Soil: Ordinary, well-drained soil.
Watering: Keep moist.
Origin: Europe.

HELIOPSIS HELIANTHOIDES
(he-li-OP-sis) ❧ **False Sunflower**

Here's a bonus for the late summer, fall garden. It looks a bit like a sunflower but not as large or coarse. I like it much better and you don't have to stake it.

Uses: It's a wonderful plant in a native garden or informal section of your garden. Great cut flower.

Maintenance: Deadheading extends the blooming season. Propagate by division every 3 to 4 years. Cuttings of roots easily done in summer. Seeds often yield uninteresting types.

Light: Tolerates shade.
Size: 60" (150 cm) high, 18" - 24" (45 cm - 60 cm) wide.

Color: Yellow blooms are bright with a darker center disk.

Blooms: July to August.
Soil: Tolerant of poor but fertile soils. Well-drained soils will result in a profusion of blooms.

Watering: Drought resistant, but responds to watering during dry spells with better flowers.

Origin: North America.

Hen-and-Chickens *see* SEMPERVIVUM TECTORUM

Houseleek *see* SEMPERVIVUM TECTORUM

HYDRANGEA ANOMALA
PETIOLARIS (hy-DRAN-jia) ❧
Climbing Hydrangea

My favorite climber, it takes a long time to establish but once done it can ramp over the worst eye-sores and transform them. It's a clinger rather than a twiner.

Uses: May extend 75' (22 m) up trees. It tolerates pollution so anyone with a garden in a built-up area can do well with this plant. If used as a screening plant, it will need strong support to carry its vigorous growth; plant near a front door to frame it; let it cover the garage or a potting shed.

Maintenance: May require initial support until aerial roots become established. Propagate in summer by cuttings under glass. Prune in spring to maintain shape and size once it's well established. Be patient—it takes about four years.

Light: Full sun to partial shade.

Size: Grows as high as 75' (22 m).

Color: Broad leaves are deep green above and downy, pale green beneath. Flowers are creamy white clusters.

Blooms: June.

Soil: Any kind of well-drained soil enriched with humus.

Watering: Keep moist in early years. Tolerates drier conditions once established.

Origin: Asia.

Jack-in-the-pulpit *see* ARISAEMA TRIPHYLLUM

Japanese Honeysuckle *see* LONICERA JAPONICA

Jupiter's-beard *see* CENTRANTHUS RUBER

Keys-of-Heaven *see* CENTRANTHUS RUBER

Kiwi *see* ACTINIDIA KOLOMIKTA

Lamb's-ears *see* STACHYS BYZANTINA

Leopard's Bane *see* DORONICUM CORDATUM

LONICERA JAPONICA (lon-ISS-er-a) ❧ **Japanese Honeysuckle**

One of those incredibly sturdy vines that can be grown anywhere. It has lots of flowers, foliage and fruit, and thrives in most areas so

well it could become a pest.

Uses: A great vine for trellises, walls, the sides of houses and growing through shrubs.

Maintenance: May choke out shrubs in milder areas where it will need sensible pruning; propagate by cuttings in summer or fall through layering or by gathering seed.

Light: Full sun.

Size: Reaches 20' (6 m).

Color: Evergreen in areas warmer than zone 4; deciduous in cold winter areas; flowers are small clusters of tubular blooms that change from white to yellow, peach to pink as they age; fruits are bright red or yellow. Birds love this vine and some varieties have a lovely scent.

L. J. 'Halliana' is one of the hardiest of these vines.

Blooms: Late spring to early fall.

Soil: Ordinary soil, well-drained with lots of manure.

Watering: Keep well watered, older plants tolerate some drought.

Origin: East Asia.

MALVA MOSCHATA (MAL-va) ❧ **Musk Mallow**

One of our most beautiful wild flowers, looks marvellous in any border. Found along roadsides and edges of meadows. If you aren't a lover of hollyhocks but want a tall flower, plant this one.

Uses: Good in borders. Ideal for planting behind dianthus or combined with chrysanthemums in a cutting garden; mass on its own for a dramatic effect.

Maintenance: Cut back to ground level in fall. Self-seeds freely. Propagate by basal cuttings or sow seeds in spring.

Light: Full sun or partial shade in hot areas.

Size: 24" - 36" (60 cm - 90 cm) high, 24" (60 cm) wide.

Color: Forms a bush of finely cut light green foliage with silky, open flowers of clear rose pink. ALBA form is pure white.

Blooms: July to September.

Soil: Well-drained, dry soil. Grows well in limestone soils.

Watering: Drought resistant.

Origin: Europe.

Masterwort *see* ASTRANTIA MAJOR

MONARDA DIDYMA (mo-NAR-da) ❧ **Bee Balm, Sweet Bergamot**

A good border herb that attracts bees and hummingbirds.

Uses: Good as border plant. Excellent in meadow gardens. The aromatic blossoms can be used to make herbal tea. Combine with other tall plants such as Shasta daisies to make a solid grouping.

Maintenance: Prone to mildew in dry soils. Deadhead. Cut back hard in fall. May become invasive. Divide in spring every two years or when it flops over from the middle. I've got one I divide almost every year, and I like the shape better than one that was let go for three years.

Light: Full sun to partial shade.

Size: 30" - 36" (75 cm - 90 cm) high, 24" (60 cm) wide.

Color: Bright green, hairy leaves on stalks crowned with large clusters of small white, pink or scarlet blooms.

Blooms: June to September.

Soil: Rich, moisture-retentive soil.

Watering: Keep moist.

Origin: North America.

Musk Mallow *see* MALVA MOSCHATA

NARCISSUS POETICUS (nar-SIS-us), ❧ **Poet's Narcissus**

One of the most attractive and fragrant of all narcissi. I like most narcissi but this is my favorite.

Uses: Excellent spring flowering bulb. Good cut flower or forced bloom. Make whole beds out of them if you have space; plant among rocks; group in clusters.

Maintenance: Plant in late summer (right up to November in the North) at a depth three times the size of the bulb. Leave clumps undisturbed until they become congested. To propagate, lift bulbs when leaves die down. Remove smaller bulbs around parent. Grade plants to size. Plant in early fall and grow in nursery bed until flowering size, after 1 to 2 years. Squirrels and gophers will avoid these bulbs so they make good companions for vulnerable bulbs such as tulips.

Light: Sun to part shade.
Size: 18" (45 cm) high.
Color: Spreading white petals (perianth) and a small yellow crimson-edged cup.
Blooms: Early spring.
Soil: Fertile humus-rich soil with moderate drainage.
Watering: Keep evenly moist. Allowing soil to dry in spring or fall inhibits growth of next year's blooms.

Origin: Europe.

OENOTHERA MISSOURENSIS (ee-no-THEE-ra) **Ozark Sundrop, Sundrop**

Blooms not only in the evening but in daytime too. A lovely fragrance.

Uses: Best grown on a site that allows for its prostrate habit; in front of the border or along the edge of a raised bed, but in a situation where you can keep it contained—it's a real spreader.

Maintenance: May stop blooming in very hot weather. But keep

*(**Zone 6**) Dr. Henry Landis, Q.C.'s wonderful fall garden has color without bloom in a successful combination of Japanese Maples and* MALUS *underplanted with a collection of miniature Spruce.*

deadheading by pulling out the limp flowers and you'll have a long run with it. Propagate by division or sow seeds in spring.

Light: Full sun.

Size: 6" - 12" (15 cm - 30 cm) high, 24" (60 cm) wide.

Color: Enormous, fragrant, lemon yellow blooms open from reddish buds in late day. Even the seed pods are attractive with sprawling dark green foliage.

O. SPECIOSA has a pink flower, greyish foliage, and blooms during the day.

Blooms: June to August.

Soil: Ordinary soils. Will tolerate thin, dry ones. Avoid damp, poorly drained soil (may cause roots to rot in winter).

Watering: Drought tolerant.

Origin: North America.

Ozark Sundrop *see* OENOTHERA MISSOURENSIS

Poet's Narcissus *see* NARCISSUS POETICUS

Rodger's Flower *see* RODGERSIA AESCULIFOLIA

RODGERSIA AESCULIFOLIA (ro-JER-sia) ❧ **Rodger's Flower**

Unusual perennial that's becoming better known for its striking bronze horse chestnut-like foliage.

Uses: Good in woodland gardens; thrives in bog and near ponds or streams; pairs well with deciduous azaleas or rhododendrons.

Maintenance: Shelter from strong winds; set rhizomes just below soil level; propagate by division in spring.

Light: Full sun to partial shade.

Size: 36" - 60" (90 cm - 150 cm) high, 24" - 30" (75 cm - 100 cm) wide.

Color: Foliage may grow to 2 feet (60 centimeters); plumes of white or pink flowers rising above the foliage are much like ASTILBE.

Blooms: July.

Soil: Moist rich soil that can be peaty bog or waterside.

Watering: Wet; water deeply in dry spells.

Origin: Asia.

SEMPERVIVUM TECTORUM (sem-per-VY-vum) ❧ **Houseleek, Hen-and-chickens**

An addictive plant—get one and you'll discover dozens and dozens of different kinds. This is the perfect plant if you've got a balcony to play with. Used to be planted on rooftops to ward off lightning and the evils of witchcraft.

Uses: Generally plant in rock gardens and walls. Grows in the narrowest of cracks; use a strawberry planter and it will eventually encrust the whole thing; ideal for a trough garden or in a special planting area.

Maintenance: Will grow in the hottest of areas against sun-baked stone. Propagate by detaching and replanting the little rosettes (offsets) almost any time. Each one you pick out will become a mother plant that sends out little babies.

Light: Full sun.

Size: 4" - 12" (10 cm - 30 cm) high, 12" - 18" (30 cm - 45 cm) wide.

Color: There is a wide range of colors in the fleshy rosettes from the pales of cucumber green with maroon tips to a deep burgundy. Reddish to pink-purple star-shaped blooms.

Blooms: July to August.

Soil: Tolerates the poorest of soils if well-drained.

Watering: Though it looks like a desert plant it isn't, so don't let it dry

out. Not particularly drought resistant.

Origin: Europe.

Shasta Daisy *see* CHRYSANTHEMUM X SUPERBUM

Spiderwort *see* TRADESCANTIA X ANDERSONIANA

Spirea *see* ASTILBE

STACHYS BYZANTINA (STA-kys) ❧ **Lamb's-ears**

Another of my favorite grey plants. It adds an element of sensual elegance no matter where you put it.

Uses: It makes an enticing ground cover; or filler in any flower bed; looks especially good with old-fashioned roses or pinks; or with irises. I especially like it combined with lavender as the edging along a walkway. Its natural companions are the other Mediterranean herbs.

Maintenance: Remove flowers after they make a good show and cut back to end of the stem, or leave them on until they fade and then cut back; in fall pull out all the dead stems; tends to rot in hot humid summers; propagate by division spring to fall.

Light: Full sun.

Size: 12" - 18" (30 cm - 45 cm) high, 12" (30 cm) wide.

Color: Velvety silver-grey foliage; leafy flowers are on white woolly spikes in mauve, pink and lilac blue.

Blooms: June to July.

Soil: Grows in almost any soil but it should be well drained.

Watering: Tolerates drought.

Origin: Turkey, Southwestern Asia.

Sundrop *see* OENOTHERA MISSOURENSIS

Sweet Bergamot *see* MONARDA DIDYMA

TRADESCANTIA X ANDERSONIANA (trad-ess-KAN-tia) ❧ **Spiderwort**

This attractive plant named after two famous plant explorers is some-times considered a weed. Not by me. It holds up to incredible amounts of pollution and usually looks quite buoyant.

Uses: Mixes well in any kind of border that requires color and the effect of long arching leaves—these tend to get scraggly so make sure you mix them in with other plants of the same height.

Maintenance: Really requires little work; if it starts to look straggly, cut it right back and perhaps you'll get regrowth; minimal water and food will keep it in check; propagate by division.

Light: Sun to partial shade.

Size: 18" - 30" (45 cm - 75 cm) high, 24" - 36" (60 cm - 90 cm) wide.

Color: From white to blue to pur-ple and magenta over strikingly ele-gant leaves.

Blooms: July to August.

Soil: Will tolerate boggy condi-tions but any soil will do, including very poor.

Watering: Needs moisture but cut back if it gets invasive.

Origin: North and South America.

Tulip *see* TULIPA TARDA

TULIPA TARDA (TEW-lip-a), ❧ **Species Tulip**

One of the loveliest of all the tulips and often overlooked for the more flashy hybrids.

Uses: Almost anywhere but especial-ly at the front of borders or in a rock garden; underneath shrubs not yet up so that fading foliage can be disguised.

Maintenance: Plant 4 inches (10 centimeters) deep and 3 inches (8 centimeters) apart in sheltered, preferably south facing, spots; lighten up heavy soils; dress with bone meal and cultivate deeply; doesn't need lift-ing; apply general fertilizer each spring; propagate from offsets formed around bulbs. Lift when foliage turns yellow; remove offsets and they'll bloom in about two years.

Light: Full sun.

Size: 4" - 6" (10 cm - 15 cm) high.

Color: Narrow slight grey-green leaves form a small clump. Up to five starry white flowers with brilliant yel-low centers.

Blooms: Early to midspring.

Soil: Light, well-drained soil.

Watering: Regular.

Origin: Asia.

TULIPA KAUFMANNIANA ❧ **Water Lily Tulip**

A marvellous species tulip that I like to grow around the edges of a tree in the front garden, with a fritillaria nearby warding off pesky squirrels.

Uses: Their compact size makes them ideal for the rock garden or any small spot you've got unused by other bulbs. You can't have too many.

Maintenance: Same as T. TARDA.

Light: Full sun.

Size: 6" - 10" (15 cm - 25 cm) high.

Color: The wide star-shaped flow-ers are creamy white flushed with red.

Blooms: Early spring.

Soil: Light, well-drained.

Watering: Regular.

Origin: Asia.

Valerian *see* CENTRANTHUS RUBER

Water Lily Tulip *see* TULIPA KAUF-MANNIANA

More plants for this zone:

AKEBIA QUINATA, **Five Leaf Akebia (vine)**
ALLIUM CHRISTOPHII, **Star-of-Persia**
ALYSSUM SAXATILE, **Basket of Gold, Gold Dust**
ANGELICA, **Angelica**
ANTENNARIA, **Pussytoes**
ASTER X FRIKARTII, **Hybrid Aster**
AUBRIETA DELTOIDEA, **Purple Rockcress**
CATANANCHE CAERULEA, **Blue Cupid's Dart**
CROCUS VERNUS, **Common Crocus**
DAPHNE CNEORUM, **Rose Daphne**
ENDYMION HISPANICUS, **Spanish Bluebell, Squill**
EPIMEDIUM X RUBRUM, **Barrenwort**
ERANTHIS HYEMALIS, **Winter Aconite**
ERINUS ALPINUS, **Fairy Foxglove**
ERYSIMUM ASPERUM, **Prairie Rocket**
EUPATORIUM PURPUREUM, **Joe-pye Weed**
GEUM X BORISII, **Avens**
LEUCOJUM AESTIVUM, **Summer Snowflake**
MUSCARI ARMENIACUM, **Grape Hyacinth**
ORNITHOGALUM UMBELLATUM, **Star of Bethlehem**
PUSCHKINIA SCILLOIDES, **Striped Squill**
TROLLIUS X HYBRIDUS, **Globeflower**

HARDINESS ZONE FIVE

This zone covers pockets in British Columbia; Central Ontario; coastal parts of the Maritimes; Eastern Seaboard of the United States; and all of Southern Quebec.

These areas have healthy snow covering, so perennials normally have good winter protection.

More can be supplied by planting in areas with some sort of shelter: snow fences in the country; a courtyard in the city. Look for plants that like cold winters and hot summers.

Much of the potentially heavy weather is leavened by the St. Lawrence River in the east and large lakes in other parts of the country. This is another zone where bulbs and perennials do exceptionally well. In different areas of the country, some Zone 5s will not grow such common shrubs as forsythia. You will have to experiment to find a cultivar suitable for your location. IRIS SIBIRICA, Siberian Iris, grows exceptionally well in this zone of cold winter temperatures. You will have to protect delicate plants with a thick cover of mulch. Check in February to see if you have to add to the mulch because of a thaw. This will help keep the ground frozen. CAREX CONICA MARGINATA, is a miniature variegated sedge—an excellent cover for bulbs. One trend is to mass grasses, planting large drifts and interweaving them with the fescues. This is an alternative to expanses of lawn which, of course gobble up huge amounts of water.

CLIMATIC CONSIDERATIONS:
Average annual minimum temperatures:
Zone 5: a. -29°C to -26°C   -20°F to -15°F
         b. -26°C to -23°C   -15°F to -10°F
Number of growing days: 210

Indicator Shrubs: COTINUS COGGYRIA, Smokebush; FORSYTHIA OVATA, Early Forsythia; VIBURNUM CARLESII, Fragrant Viburnum
These plants indicate what will grow at the edge of a zone and will give you more information about hardiness in your area

(Zone 6) Lisa Dalholt has capitalized on the feeling of a Victorian cottage and reflected it in her front garden. This is an ideal blend of garden and architecture. The rose on the left is Blaze; the pot contains BEGONIA; *behind on the left: Daylilies;* DELPHINIUM; DIANTHUS BARBATUS, *Sweet William;* SAGINA SUBULATA, *Scotch Moss; Corkscrew Hazelnut;* THALICTRUM; ACHILLEA *Cerise Queen;* VERONICA SPICATA.

SELECTED LISTINGS
FOR HARDINESS ZONE FIVE

ANDROSACE CARNEA
(an-DROSS-as-ee) ❧ **Rock Jasmine**
Belongs to the primrose family; small tufted herbs grown in rock gardens or in places where one can appreciate their exquisite rosettes.

Uses: Its small size makes it ideal for rock and trough gardens.

Maintenance: Cover immediate surroundings with pebbles or pea gravel; propagate by division in fall or spring, or detach rosettes and grow them in a cold frame in summer.

Light: Full sun.

Size: 4" - 6" (10 cm - 15 cm) high, 8" (20 cm) wide.

Color: Tight rosettes with pink to off-white blooms.

Blooms: May to June.

Soil: Loose pebbly, neutral to acid.

Watering: Moderately wet.

Origin: Europe.

Blue Flax *see* LINUM PERENNE

CLEMATIS (KLEM-at-is) ❧
An extremely varied genus. One of the most popular and showy climbers with over 100 species cultivated in North America alone. Try as many as you have room for.

Uses: An outstanding vine for summer screening; for the wild garden; train up trees or let it ramp through host shrubs. Try it as a container plant if you have a small garden. Non-clinging types make good ground covers, especially around roses.

Maintenance: Plant between autumn and spring; put flat stones over roots at base to keep them shaded, then grow plants nearby that will shade them as they get older. They need to be supported: mesh, chicken wire; shrub, tree or other vine. If you do the latter make sure the clematis is a foot away from the base and has a large well-groomed hole, full of compost and good soil in which to rest (at least 18 inches [45 centimeters] square). Train young plants by tying to a slender stick. You can propagate them by layering or taking cuttings in summer. If you deadhead C. JACKMANII, for instance, you'll get a second bloom in late summer.

Pruning: This is important. When you decide to buy clematis, find out what category it's in:

Group 1: species including C. MONTANA, C. ALPINA and C. MACROPETALA produce flowers from old stems so don't prune until blooming is completed. Once they're over 16 feet (5 meters) merely cut out any weak or dead stems.

Group 2: Large flowered hybrids such as C. PATENS 'Nelly Moser' cut back to a strong pair of buds when they become visible in early spring.

Group 3: C. JACKMANII produces flowers on new stems each year; cut back to base of previous season's growth within 12 inches (30 centimeters) of soil in early spring. These can be grown in Zone 3.

Light: Shade roots; let stems and flowers get full sun.

Size: From 12' - 30' (3.5 m - 9 m) high.

Color: Flowers range from tiny star-like shapes to big relaxed circular blooms, from white, yellow, red, blue, purple and pink.

Blooms: July to fall.

Soil: Cool moist, shaded soil; neutral to alkaline with average fertility, good drainage.

Watering: They like lots of water.

Origin: Asia, Europe, North America.

Common Rue *see* RUTA GRAVE-OLENS

CORYDALIS (ko-ry-DAL-is) ❧
This relative of bleeding heart forms low leafy mounds of foliage with delicate flowers making it a valuable foliage plant.

Uses: I like this one in dappled shade and in a woodland garden; it will even grow between paving stones and cracks in old walls. Does spectacularly in the Pacific Northwest. Think of it mainly as a foliage plant.

Maintenance: Clip plants back after flowering to keep them in a compact form and to prevent self-seeding which they will do with great abandon; propagate by seeds in spring.

Light: Full sun to full shade.

Size: 12" - 15" (30 cm - 40 cm) high, 12" (30 cm) wide.

Color: Yellow blooms. C. CAVA has purple-pink flowers

Blooms: Early spring.

Soil: Light well-drained soil that doesn't dry out.

Watering: Keep moist.

Origin: Europe and Asia.

(Zone 5) Amy Stewart lets CLEMATIS POTANINII *ramp over the tool shed with profligate abandon.*

Crown Imperial *see* FRITILLARIA IMPERIALIS

ERYNGIUM MARITIMUM
(e-RINJ-ium) ❧ **Sea Holly**
The flowers, which resemble those of the thistle, make this an interesting plant. As a starter plant, it has the great virtue of growing in any soil.
Uses: Useful as cut or dried blooms. You probably won't want masses of this one so think of it as a specimen. Fit it in with other plants about the same size and it will add an air of mystery. Especially good with any grey foliage plant.
Maintenance: Doesn't like wet winter conditions; use a gravel mulch around the crown and don't disturb the roots; cut flower stems down to the ground in late winter; propagate by root cutting in late winter or by seeds in spring.
Light: Full sun.
Size: 24" - 36" high, 12" wide.
Color: Stiff leathery leaves with thistle-like blue flowers on blue-green foliage.
Blooms: July to September.
Soil: Will tolerate poor soil, if well drained; if the soil is too rich it's liable to become unmanageable and flop over.
Watering: Drought resistant.
Origin: Mediterranean.

FRITILLARIA IMPERIALIS
(frit-ill-AY-ria) ❧ **Crown Imperial**
A most exotic and rather strange looking creature that's been cultivated since the 16th century.
Uses: Striking in back of the border with plants such as white narcissi and erythronium; squirrels hate its skunky smell (never store in the refrigerator if you can't plant immediately) and will avoid anything nearby. Plant tulips all around and you might save them from these pests.
Maintenance: This is a plant that doesn't like to be moved so make sure you have it in the right place when you start out. Propagate by fresh seeds under glass in summer or by offsets removed in dormant season.
Light: Full sun to light shade.
Size: 36" (90 cm) high, 9" - 15" (25 cm - 40 cm) wide.
Color: Leafy at base then bare stems up to the large clusters of bell flowers of yellow, orange and scarlet.
Blooms: Early spring.
Soil: Fertile, well-drained. Waterlogged soil is fatal.
Watering: Ordinary applications.
Origin: Persia.

FRITILLARIA MELEAGRIS
(frit-ill-AY-ria) ❧ **Snake's-head**
A bulbous perennial in the Lily family originating in moist meadows.

It's an easy-to-grow perennial.

Uses: Good in wild or meadow gardens. Looks beautiful in uncut grass, in an undisturbed border, or peat garden; cluster under a BETULA PENDULA 'Youngii', Weeping Birch.

Maintenance: Naturalize in short grass. Propagate by seed or by bulbils from lifted plants. It takes several years to reach flowering size.

Light: Full sun to light shade.

Size: 12" (30 cm) high, 6" (15 cm) wide.

Color: Large drooping bells of purple. A few narrow grey-green leaves give a slender appearance.

Blooms: Early spring to May.

Soil: Ordinary fertile soil.

Watering: Keep moist.

Origin: California.

GENTIANA ASCLEPIADEA (jen-she-AY-na) ❧ **Willow Gentian**

This is another large genus: special for its intense blue flowers.

Uses: Best in a rock or alpine garden or a shady spot.

Maintenance: Prefers cool conditions; propagate by seed in fall or spring in a cold frame; division in early spring or basal cutting later.

Light: Partial to full shade.

Size: 12" - 36" (30 cm - 90 cm) high, 24" (60 cm) wide.

Color: Blue trumpet with white throat on arching stems; horizontal leaves look like those of the willow.

Blooms: July to August.

Soil: Moist loamy, acid soil.

Watering: Keep very moist.

Origin: Europe.

GALTONIA CANDICANS (gawl-TOE-nia) ❧ **Summer Hyacinth**

One of the many wonderful summer bulbs, it's a treat in the August garden.

Uses: Effective background for a sunny border, combines well with hostas which will cover up the aftermath of blooming; mix in with medium-sized plants with more ferny foliage such as THALICTRUM, AQUILEGIA.

Maintenance: Leave undisturbed; cut faded stems back to the ground in fall—like other bulbs the foliage provides next year's food; mulch heavily in winter or lift bulbs in the fall; propagate from offsets when dormant or by seed in spring; offsets can be stored over winter and planted in spring.

Light: Full sun.

Size: 36" - 48" (90 cm - 120 cm) high.

Color: Pure white pendulous bell-like flowers on the tall stalk; rises above straplike leaves.

Blooms: July and August.

Soil: Deep fertile, well-drained but moisture-retentive soil.

Watering: Keep well watered in dry spells.

Origin: South Africa.

Golden Groundsel *see* LIGULARIA DENTATA

Herb-of-Grace *see* RUTA GRAVEOLENS

(Zone 5) This breathtaking border is in Amy Stewart's garden.
Left to right: HEMEROCALLIS *'Hyperion', Yellow Daylily;*
FILIPENDULA RUBRA, *Meadowsweet;* LILIUM *'Copper King';*
LIGULARIA; IRIS SIBIRICA, *Siberian Iris;*
foreground: PHLOX PANICULATA *'Mia Ruys'.*

HIBISCUS SYRIACUS (hy-BISK-us)
⚘ Rose-of-Sharon

An old-fashion shrub grown in North America since colonial times.

Uses: Grows well near the seashore, looks better mixed with other tall plants rather than as a specimen; can be a good fall plant if you get the right color. I learned to appreciate a pink that I thought quite vile at first for its combination of dark buds with lighter flowers.

Maintenance: Remove frost-damaged tips in spring; young plants may not need protection but it's a good idea to mulch anyway; to propagate take heel cuttings. Deadhead on a regular basis. This one has been spoiled by hybridizers so try to find someone who has the older single ones if you can. They grow easily from seed.

Light: Full sun.

Size: 8' (2.5 m) high, 5' (1.5 m) wide.

Color: Rich green leaves in spring, with later blooms of pure white to blue, purplish-red, violet, pink and red. Over a number of years, this plant may revert to its species color and your blue plant may end up white.

Blooms: August to first frost.

Soil: Well-drained humus-rich soil.

Watering: Moderately wet.

Origin: Asia.

Lavender Cotton *see* SANTOLINA CHAMAECYPARISSUS

LIGULARIA DENTATA (lig-yew-LAY-ria) ⚘ **Golden Groundsel**

A wonderful architectural plant with large flowers and lustrous foliage.

Uses: Usually grown in bog gardens.

If you keep the soil moist it will thrive in a regular border; most suitable by a pond or stream; great companion to skunk cabbage; good specimen for the back of a border.

Maintenance: Keep mulched and fertilized; cut back to near ground in late fall; propagate by division every three years in spring which will help contain spread.

Light: Full sun to partial shade.

Size: 36" - 48" (90 cm - 120 cm) high, 24" - 36" (60 cm - 90 cm) wide.

Color: Big orange-red dark-eyed daisyish flowers on leafy foliage. L. D. 'Desdemona,' smaller more compact version.

L. STENOCEPHALA 'The Rocket,' a more refined hybrid.

Blooms: July or August.

Soil: Deep rich, moist soil or in bog or damp woodland soil.

Watering: Keep very moist and water deeply in dry spells.

Origin: East Asia.

LINUM PERENNE (LY-num)
⚘ Blue Flax

A cheerful but short-lived plant that lightens up the dense part of a border.

Uses: An airy, delicate plant for an informal garden or a meadow.

Maintenance: Mulch over the winter in cold areas; this is a great little self-seeder; propagate by seed in spring or take cuttings in spring.

Light: Full sun.

Size: 12" - 24" (30 cm - 60 cm) high, 18" (45 cm) wide.

Color: Yellow or blue with blue-green narrow leaves; flowers open on sunny days.

Blooms: June to July.

Soil: Well-drained.

Watering: Drought resistant.

Origin: Europe.

Meadow Rue *see* THALICTRUM ROCHEBRUNIANUM

Moss campion *see* SILENE ACAULIS

Ornamental Rhubarb *see* RHEUM PALMATUM

Prairie Mallow *see* SIDALCEA MALVIFLORA

RHEUM PALMATUM (REE-um)
⚘ Ornamental Rhubarb

Highly prized as a foliage plant whose jagged edged leaves unfold to about two to three feet across. Not for small gardens.

Uses: A good plant near ponds and streams. Use it as a specimen for a dramatic accent; or at the end of a garden as a focal point for a vista.

Maintenance: Cut faded flower stems back to base. Propagate by division in dormant season or by seed in spring. Mulch base to keep roots cool.

Light: Full sun to partial shade.

Size: 6' - 10' (1.8 m - 3 m) high, 4'- 6' (1.2 m - 1.8 m) wide.

Color: Beautiful red foliage when open, turning to green after flowering. Crimson flowers produce attractive seed capsules.

Blooms: June.

Soil: Ordinary soil enriched by humus.

Watering: Requires a lot of moisture. Water deeply in dry spells.

Origin: Siberia and Asia.

(Zone 5)Amy Stewart's rock garden has the same sort of romantic spirit as the rest of her garden: THYMUS LANUGINOSA, *Woolly Thyme;* CAMPANULA *Blue Clips;* T. SERPYLLUM; *Dianthus;* CORYDALIS LUTEA; C. PORTENSCHLAGIANA. *In the urn:* VERBENA, HELICHRYSUM PETIOLATUM.

(Zone 5) Betty Piper's lovely old steps leading down to the river are planted in a profusion of SEDUM; CONVALLARIA, *Lily-of-the-valley; and* EUPHORBIA.

SANTOLINA CHAMAECYPARISSUS (san-to-LY-na) ❧ **Lavender Cotton**

One of my favorite plants, especially mixed with herbs; a small shrubby plant with aromatic leaves when crushed.

Uses: Good ground cover on poor or gravelly soils; works wonders as a low clipped hedge instead of BUXUS, Box; beautiful at the edge of any border.

Maintenance: Prune stiffly in spring and after flowering to keep it in shape either as a ground cover, hedge, or round specimen. Set hedging plants 15 inches (40 centimeters) apart; propagate by cuttings taken in late summer.

Light: Full sun.

Size: 18" (45 cm) high, 24" (60 cm) wide.

Color: One of the best of the silver plants. Don't grow it for the flowers which are an insignificant yellow like the button of a daisy.

Blooms: July to August.

Soil: Well-drained; tolerates poor sandy soil.

Watering: Requires very little.

Origin: Europe (Mediterranean).

Sea Holly *see* ERYNGIUM MARITIMUM

Rock Jasmine *see* ANDROSACE CARNEA

Rose-of-Sharon *see* HIBISCUS SYRIACUS

RUTA GRAVEOLENS (ROO-ta) ❧ **Common Rue, Herb-of-Grace**

An evergreen sub-shrub noted for its medicinal disinfectant properties but mostly valued for its handsome foliage.

Uses: Cool lacy foliage at the edge of a border.

Maintenance: Wear gloves when handling; foliage may cause dermatitis; prune back in spring to force bushiness; prone to legginess; propagate by cuttings under glass in late summer.

Light: Full sun.

Size: 24" - 36" (60 cm - 90 cm) high, 18" (45 cm) wide.

Color: Bright almost sulphur yellow blooms that aren't particularly interesting; pungent odor; foliage is blue-green. R. G. 'Jackman's Blue' is more important as a foliage plant.

Blooms: June to August.

Soil: Ordinary well-drained soil.

Watering: Tolerates dry conditions.

Origin: Europe.

SIDALCEA MALVIFLORA (sy-DAL-sea) ❧ **Prairie Mallow**

Somewhat like a miniature hollyhock, this plant is a striking addition to the garden and has a strong vertical effect without looking weedy.

Uses: Makes a fine border plant. Surround with silvery foliage plants or the metallic blue flowers of ERYNGIUM. If you have a cutting garden, make sure you include this one.

Maintenance: Tall cultivars need staking. Deadhead to encourage second bloom. Cut stems back to base in fall. Propagate by division in spring.

Light: Full sun to partial shade.

Size: 24" - 48" (60 cm - 120 cm) high, 18" (45 cm) wide.
Color: Handsome foliage. Spikes of satiny flowers of a variable pink.
Blooms: June to September.
Soil: Deep, fertile loamy soil.
Watering: Ordinary.
Origin: North America.

SILENE ACAULIS (sy-LEE-ne)
❧ **Moss Campion**

I love this sprightly plant which is a member of the pink family. An easy alpine plant with a long flowering period.

Uses: Good for edges of borders; rock garden plant. I like them running through the border adding a bit of brightness when other things are starting to look ragged at the edges.
Maintenance: Plant spreads slowly and roots resent disturbance. Propagation is best and easiest from seed sown in spring. You can also propagate from stem cuttings in summer grown under glass.
Light: Full sun to light shade.
Size: 6" (15 cm) high, 12" (30 cm) wide.
Color: Spring leaves are apple green with magenta pink blooms.
Blooms: August to September.
Soil: Adapts to any soil from sand to clay, preferring deep, well-drained soils.
Watering: Do not allow to dry out.
Origin: Europe.

Snake's-head *see* FRITILLARIA MELEAGRIS

Summer Hyacinth *see* GALTONIA CANDICANS

TEUCRIUM CHAMAEDRYS
(TEW-krium) ❧ **Wall Germander**
A herb of the sage family with leathery green foliage; purple or white clusters of flowers.
Uses: Excellent rock and wall plant, ground cover, and edging; fragrant.

Maintenance: In northern gardens plants benefit from wall shelter; shear back to keep neat after blooming; reduce vigorous shoots by up to one-half; propagate by cuttings grown under glass in late spring.
Light: Full sun, tolerates some shade.
Size: 12" - 24" (30 cm - 60 cm) high, 12" - 24" (30 cm - 60 cm) wide.
Color: Dark green crinkly foliage with spikes of lavender-pink to purple flowers.
Blooms: July to September.
Soil: Any well-drained soil.
Watering: Tolerates dry conditions.
Origin: Europe.

THALICTRUM ROCHEBRUNIANUM (thal-IK-trum) ❧ **Meadow Rue**
An elegant plant with sprays of beautiful leaves that resemble maidenhair fern in some varieties and AQUILEGIA in others. Delicate flowers.
Uses: Looks wonderful with deep blue delphiniums and Michaelmas daisies; use near heavily leafed shrubs such as viburnum or to mask the fading of DICENTRA, Bleeding Heart.
Maintenance: Needs wind protection; tall varieties will probably need staking; over-fertilizing causes weak growth; propagate by seeds in summer. Cut off blooms when they are finished and enjoy the foliage.
Light: Full sun to partial shade.
Size: 36" - 60" (90 cm - 150 cm) high, 18" - 24" (45 cm - 60 cm) wide.
Color: Blue-grey foliage that turns a delicate yellow in fall; flowers range from a lemon yellow to a soft burgundy.

T. AQUILEGIFOLIUM has lilac colored flowers. T. Hewitt's Double is a lighter color of violet.
Blooms: July to August.
Soil: Ordinary soil, humus-enriched.
Watering: Requires lots of moisture.
Origin: Europe.

Wall Germander *see* TEUCRIUM CHAMAEDRYS

Willow Gentian *see* GENTIANA ASCLEPIADEA

More plants you should consider planting in Zone 5:

ALLIUM KARATAVIENSE
ANCHUSA AZUREA, **Italian Bugloss**
CAMASSIA LEICHTLINII, **Quamash**
CELASTRUS SCANDENS, **Bittersweet**
COLCHICUM, **Autumn Crocus**
CROCUS TOMASINIANUS
DRABA BRYOIDES, **Whitlow Grass**
ERYTHRONIUM, **Fawn-lily**
HEDERA HELIX, **Ivy**
HELIANTHEMUM NUMMULARIUM, **Sun Rose**
IPOMOEA TRICOLOR, **Morning Glory**
LEONTOPODIUM ALPINUM, **Edelweiss**
LOBELIA SIPHILITICA, **Great Blue Lobelia**
POTENTILLA ATROSANGUINEA, **Himalayan Cinquefoil**
PRUNELLA, **Self-heal**
RANUNCULUS ACONITIFOLIUS, **Aconite Buttercup**
STOKESIA LAEVIS, **Stokes' Aster**

HARDINESS ZONE SIX

*I*n the central part of the continent, Zone 6 ranges through the once vast deciduous forests. The shade and light are dappled and provide welcome relief from the blistering heat that seems to visit these areas, especially during July and August.

Much of Zone 6 hovers in swathes around the Great Lakes. There is a leavening effect from those vast bodies of water as well as an often unwelcome supply of humidity. Plants from North China, Korea and Manchuria behave more like plants from North America, and do better, than many of the European and western Asian species. That is why it's always a good idea to know where your plants originated, especially if they're expensive shrubs and ornamentals.

Along the East Coast, the soil is of prime consideration. It's highly acidic and supports such a wide range of spectacular plants that those of us without it are quite jealous. If it's necessary to have a slightly more neutral soil, add lime and well-rotted compost when you dig in your plants. Properly applied it will last about two years (see page 54 for more on changing the pH of soil).

A much better route to follow is to pick the right plant for the site. If it's a windy spot, as so many are on the coast, find plants that won't be slaughtered by one ferocious storm—Pacific Giant Delphiniums for instance. Look for shorter, sturdier varieties.

Acid soil welcomes ericaceous plants: rhododendrons, heathers, azaleas and the dozens of other stunningly beautiful plants. Check all the listings for acid-loving plants.

CLIMATIC CONSIDERATIONS:
Average annual minimum temperatures:
-10°F to 0°F   -23°C to -18°C
Number of growing days: 225 days

Indictor Shrubs: ACER PALMATUM, Japanese Maple; DEUTZIA GRACILIS, Slender Deutzia; FORSYTHIA X INTERMEDIA 'Spectabilis', Showy Forsythia.

(Zone 9) PAEONIA, *Peonies and* DELPHINIUM *are graceful companions in Al and Shirley Smith's border.*

SELECTED LISTINGS
FOR HARDINESS ZONE SIX

ANEMONE(an-EM-on-e)
❧ **Windflower**

Perennial herb with bright colored flowers. Durable attractive foliage. A. DE CAEN favored by florists for early spring bouquets.

Uses: Ideal for the front of borders; cut flowers.

A. BLANDA belongs in the rockery or woodland garden.

A. JAPONICA is one of the major bright spots of the late summer garden.

Maintenance: Best in coastal areas; mulch heavily in winter in other areas; keep out of the midday sun and divide every 3 to 4 years; soak tubers and rhizomes several hours before planting.

Light: Full sun to light shade.

Size: 6" - 12" (15 cm - 30 cm) high, 12" - 24" (30 cm -60 cm) wide. A. JAPONICA grows from 3' (90 cm) to 5' (150 cm) tall.

Color: There are several species.

A. CORONARIA (zone 7) has rich red, purple, blue and white blooms.

A. BLANDA has riveting all-white flowers.

A. PULSATILLA bell-shaped blue or red-purple blooms in early spring followed by interesting fluffy seed heads.

A. JAPONICA ranges from a pure white to shades of pink.

Blooms: A. CORONARIA, early spring to fall.

A. PULSATILLA, early spring.

A. BLANDA, early spring self-seeders.

A. JAPONICA, late summer or early fall.

Soil: Well-drained, organically rich.

Watering: Keep moist.

Origin: Southern Europe.

ANTHERICUM LILIAGO (an-THER-ik-um) ❧ **St. Bernard's Lily**

An ideal flower arranger's plant with starry white blooms. A very elegant plant.

Uses: Cut flowers, fragrant; pairs well with CHEIRANTHUS, **Wallflower,** OR ARMERIA MARITIMA, **Thrift;** most effective massed on its own.

Maintenance: Don't disturb this plant; mulch in spring with organic material; in northern gardens tuberous roots should be dried and stored over winter; divide any crowded clumps in spring or after flowering; seeds might not come true.

Light: Full sun to partial shade.

Size: 36" (90 cm) high, 12" (30 cm) wide.

Color: Grey-green linear leaves 12 inches (30 centimeters), with a long stalk and white flowers. Forms clumps. A great favorite of Gertrude Jekyll.

Blooms: May to June.

Soil: Rich and moist but light.

Watering: Keep moist.

Origin: Europe.

COREOPSIS VERTICILLATA 'Moonbeam' (ko-rea-OP-sis)
❧ **Threadleaf Coreopsis**

One of the finest perennials. A great starter plant.

Uses: Excellent cut flower, good for the front of a border.

Maintenance: Can be invasive; low supports may be needed in windy areas; cut dead flower stalks at base to encourage more blooms; propagate by division in spring.

Light: Full sun.

Size: 12" - 36" (30 cm - 90 cm) high, 24" (60 cm) wide.

Color: Fernlike leaves form a twiggy bush with vivacious daisylike flowers.

Blooms: June to fall.

Soil: Tolerates any soil, needs good drainage.

Watering: Drought resistant.

Origin: North America.

EUPHORBIA (Yew-FOR-bia)
❧ **Spurge**

A large and very diverse genus that covers weeds to poinsettias. Named after the first-century Roman physician Euphorbus. All have poisonous milky white sap.

Uses: Useful anywhere a handsome plant is required: in a border, rock garden or as a potted plant.

Maintenance: A long lived plant; disease and pest free; always use gloves when handling since the sap is toxic; may need shelter and mulch in cold areas; cut flower shoots off at the base after blooming; propagate by seeds in spring.

Light: Full sun to part shade.

Size: 6" - 60" (15 cm - 150 cm) high, 12" - 36" (30 cm - 90 cm) wide.

Color: Individual flowers are not as significant as the colorful bracts that surround them: E. GRIFFITHII, red bracts with grey-green foliage; E. POLYCHROMA, dark green leaves topped with bright bracts that look like tiny jewels; E. MYRSINITES, glaucus foliage with yellow bracts; E.

(Zone 5) Amy Stewart's steps are graced by EUPHORBIA MYRSINITES, *Myrtle Spurge.*

CYPARISSIAS, yellowish bracts turn red when they ripen.

Blooms: Early spring to midsummer.

Soil: Well-drained, poor to medium soil.

Watering: Tolerates dry conditions.

Origin: Africa, Europe and North America.

Himalayan Blue Poppy *see* MECONOPSIS BETONICIFOLIA

LAVANDULA ANGUSTIFOLIA (lav-AN-dew-la) ❧ **English Lavender**

My favorite herb—can't have too many in a garden. There are several cultivars so start a collection.

Uses: The leaves and flowers are used in potpourri (remove before they come into full bloom to retain the special oil, let dry and the scent will last for years); grow in herb gardens, English cottage gardens, rock gardens; or use as a low clipped hedge. A wonderful container plant with the true GERANIUM, Cranesbill; combined with stachys it makes a soft, romantic edging to even the dullest walkway or edge of border.

Maintenance: For hedge plants place 10 inches (25 centimeters) to 12 inches (30 centimeters) apart; cut back deadheads to end of the flower stalk—then cut back from there for clippings; propagate by clippings taken in late summer—stick them in individual pots and keep in a cold frame over winter; transplant after flowering; prune lightly in spring.

Light: Full sun.

Size: 36" (90 cm) high, 12" - 36" (30 cm - 90 cm) wide.

Color: A gorgeous silver-grey foliage with dense spikes of clear blue to purple blooms.

Blooms: July to August.

Soil: Requires good drainage, humus-rich soil.

Watering: Drought tolerant.

Origin: Southern Europe, North Africa.

Lavender *see* LAVANDULA ANGUSTIFOLIA

LEWISIA COTYLEDON (lew-ISS-ia) ❧

Member of the portulaca family. Striking flowers and temperamental habits.

Uses: In rockeries, on walls and in alpine or trough gardens; also as pot plants.

Maintenance: Plant on slopes or vertical crevices to ensure proper drainage; mulch around collar with gravel or crushed stone 1 inch (2.5 centimeters) to 2 inches (5 centimeters) deep; a dry period after flowering is essential; propagate by detaching rosettes and growing in cold frame during summer; by seed or division in spring.

Light: Partial shade.

Size: 9" - 12" (13 cm - 30 cm) high, 16" (25 cm) wide.

Color: Evergreen leaves with crinkled edges and stunning crimson, pink or white flowers.

Blooms: June to July.

Soil: Absolutely must have perfect drainage; planting on a slope is best. When grown in pots needs gritty loam with coarse leaf mould and a light dressing of bone meal.

Watering: Does not like any winter damp.

Origin: North America.

London Pride see SAXIFRAGA UMBROSA

MECONOPSIS BETONICIFOLIA (mek-on-OP-sis) ❧**Himalayan Blue Poppy**
The famous Himalayan Blue Poppy, M. BETONICIFOLIA, is usually designated for zone 7. It really isn't supposed to grow anywhere other than the warm Pacific Northwest, but determined growers have brought it along in almost every zone including the harsh one in Edmonton's Devonian Botanical gardens. It's worth a try.

Uses: Does well in mild, moist parts of the garden.

Maintenance: Light shade brings out its purest blue; likes humid air; propagate by seed sown in spring when ripe; dislikes hot summers.

Light: Partial shade.

Size: 36" - 60" (90 cm - 150 cm) high, 18" (45 cm) wide.

Color: Clumps of dark green hairy leaves with clear blue flowers. Each stem may produce a dozen blooms with gold stamens. Other forms: M. CAMBRICA, Welsh Poppy has yellow flowers; M. SUPERBA, white flowers, monocarpic.

Blooms: June to July.

Soil: Ordinary humus-rich acidic soil.

*(**Zone 6**) Walter Ostrom's magnificent foliage garden proves how sensual this kind of gardening is—it doesn't need blooms. All the elements are in the leaves. From left to right:* ARCTOSTAPHYLOS UVA-URSI; *a mixture of* JUNIPERUS HORIZONTALIS; ERICA *'Springwood White' and* RHODODENDRON IMPEDITUM; *Dwarf* CALLUNA; R. IMPEDITUM; CALLUNA *variety C.W.;* R. *'Princess Ann';* R. FERRUGINEUM; R. YAKUSIMANUM; *mixtures of* JUNIPERUS PROCUMBENS *'Nana',* CALLUNA; VACCINIUM MYRTILLOIDES *(wild low bush blueberry), and* R. LEPIDOTUM; *by path,* PICEA ABIES 'NIDIFORMIS'; JUNIPERUS SQUAMATA *'Blue Star';* LEIOPHYLLUM BUXIFOLIUM.

(Zone 9) Shirley and Al Smith have developed a colorful border outside their house. The stand on the right side of the photograph is MECONOPSIS, *Himalayan Blue Poppy, and to the left is* PYRETHRUM, *Painted Daisy; in the background, peonies and delphiniums.*

Watering: Keep moist.
Origin: Asia.

PELTIPHYLLUM PELTATUM
(pel-ti-FILL-um) ❧ **Umbrella Plant**
A delightful almost exotic foliage for good autumn color. Wonderful as this plant is, it isn't recommended for small gardens.
Uses: Good bog plant, does well beside ponds and streams.
Maintenance: Grows by rhizomes so propagate by division in its dormant season.
Light: Full sun to partial shade.
Size: 24" - 48" (60 cm - 120 cm) high, 24" - 36" (60 cm - 90 cm) wide.
Color: Primarily a foliage plant with magnificent leaves that grow up to 2 feet (60 centimeters) across and turn bronzy pink in fall. Flowers are a pinkish white. P. 'Nanum' is a dwarf form 12 inches (30 centimeters) high.
Blooms: Early spring.
Soil: Moisture-retentive enriched with humus.

Watering: Keep moist.
Origin: North America.

Saint Bernard's Lily see ANTHERICUM LILIAGO

SAXIFRAGA UMBROSA
(SAX-if-ra-ga), ❧ **London Pride**
A tough perennial that can adapt to the least hospitable parts of a rock garden.
Uses: Rock garden; edging plant or ground cover on a small scale; trough garden.
Maintenance: Propagate by detaching non-flowering side rosettes in late summer and treating them as cuttings; cut off the flowers after bloom is over.
Light: Partial to full shade.
Size: 12" - 18" (30 cm - 45 cm) high, 12" (30 cm) wide.
Color: Wide rosettes of dark green fleshy leaves overhung by masses of star-shaped pink flowers.
Blooms: May to June.
Soil: Any well-drained soil, best in rocky limestone.
Watering: Keep moist.
Origin: Europe.

Spurge see EUPHORBIA

Threadleaf see COREOPSIS VERTICILLATA 'MOONBEAM'

Umbrella Plant see PELTIPHYLLUM PELTATUM

Windflower see ANEMONE

More plants you should consider for this zone:

AETHIONEMA X WARLEYENSE, **Warley Rose**
CAMPSIS GRANDIFLORA, **Trumpet Vine**
CRAMBE MARITIMA, **Sea-kale**
CYTISUS X KEWENSIS, **Broom**
HYACINTHUS ORIENTALIS
HYPERICUM OLYMPICUM, **St. John's Wort**
INCARVILLEA DELAVAYI, **Delavy Incarvillea**
LIRIOPE MUSCARI, **Big Blue Lily-turf**
LITHODOR DIFFUSA (formerly LITHOSPERMUM DIFFUSUM)
VERBASCUM X HYBRIDUM, **Mullein**
VIOLA CORNUTA, **Horned Violet**
V. ODORATA, **Sweet Violet**

HARDINESS ZONES SEVEN, EIGHT AND NINE

Anyone who lives in these zones considers themselves to be most blessed. The range of plants includes just about everything in this book. Even in zone 7, exotic plants can be protected in winter and come through unscathed. With the exception of small blips in the middle of the country, most notably in southern and southwestern Ontario, these are the zones of the Pacific Northwest down to Oregon. Plus any microclimates that you might find lurking about in your own garden.

As experienced gardeners are quick to point out, the warmest parts of the west coast marine climate on the southern tip of Vancouver Island are not like England at all. August is very dry and by September trees and plants are hardening off for winter. October in Victoria is arid; shrubs have ripened their wood and dried off, dormancy is coming along. November brings in moist air attended by fogs and winds. Even

---

CLIMATIC CONSIDERATIONS:
Average annual minimum temperatures:

Zone 7:	-18°C to -12°C	5°F to 10°F
Zone 8:	-12°C to -7°C	10°F to 20°F
Zone 9:	-7°C to -1°C	20°F to 30°F

Number of growing days:

Zone 7: 255	Zone 8: 270	Zone 9: 330

Indicator Shrubs:

7: BUXUS SEMPERVIRENS, English box; HYPERICUM HOOKERANUM 'Hidcote'; PRUNUS LAUROCERASUS, Cherry Laurel

8: AUCUBA JAPONICA, Japanese Aucuba; PERNETTYA MUCRONATA, Chilean Pernettya; VIBURNUM TINUS LAURUSTINUS

9: CRYPTOMERIA JAPONICA 'Elegans', Plum Cryptomeria; LAURUS NOBILIS, Sweet Bay, Laurel; PIERIS FORRESTII, Chinese Pieris

---

(Zone 8) Don Armstrong fits an old birdbath into his backyard landscaping. It holds sedums surrounded by geraniums and ground covers such as EPIMEDIUM and VANCOUVERIA.

though there's enough cold for bulbs, roses can last until Christmas. The first few weeks of January is the only really cold period. Then spring's on its way. But a dry wind coming off the water, warming as it rises, pulling cold air off the sea, taking all moisture with it, will dry out a border in no time at all.

There is a tradition of growing unusual plants in these areas partly because they are available and partly because the network of gardeners is so well developed. Every garden we were in had plants from other gardeners. And some of the best nurseries in North America are to be found in Oregon.

This is the land where things grow with great profligacy. It's not quite put-a-stick-in-the-ground-and-it'll-grow, but getting close. There is a passion unmatched anywhere else in the country for large expanses of grass, manicured to a fare-thee-well. It's such an easy thing to do in this climate.

The shade here is quite different from the dappled light of the east. This is the shade of the coniferous forest—consistently dense. The broad-leaf evergreen luscious rhododendron thrives in the acid soil of the rain forest. Nowhere else except along the eastern coast is there such a large selection of rhododendrons—both native and Asian. Thirty-year-old plants inundate the landscape in spring. Little shrubs become giants. They tend to overwhelm all except the most carefully designed gardens. Something gardeners everywhere should be aware of—plants grow and change their shape a lot faster than you think. Always keep in mind that the medium you're working with is extremely fluid. It takes about two years to make a good show and another three before a garden really settles down and matures. By the time this takes place a lot has happened. Especially in a climate that is so forgiving, so friendly to perennials as in these zones.

Apart from rhododendrons, ACER PALMATUM, Japanese Maples, are signatures of the west coast garden. An incredible variety of magnolias give even the most ordinary garden a gracious look. NANDINA DOMESTICA, Heavenly Bamboo, stands beside doorways for good luck according to the Japanese tradition. Exotic looking gunneras and PELTYPHYLLUM PELTATUM add another element to the densely planted gardens.

ACANTHUS grows well here, eucalyptus is a regular; OSMANTHUS, a Mediterranean looking plant much like a bay tree, also adds distinction to gardens. Hebes do well even though they suffer terribly in bad winters; however, they generally come back from the roots. What most gardeners try to avoid in this atmosphere is the dark shape of the pointy coniferous tree. CEANOTHUS 'Gloire de Versailles,' a form of wild California lilac, softens the hard edges of conifers. Be sure to cut it back or it will take over.

Water in every form dominates the coast. The rainfall can be as high as 80 inches (200 centimeters) in some parts of the lower mountain ranges. Ocean air creates mild winters, cool summers, and a long growing season. The sea acts as a great storage bank of warmth. It's an unusual winter that will bring freezing temperatures and snow. When that happens, as it did during the winter of 1989, there's incredible damage to plants.

Other climate considerations:

❧ Cool summers mean it's wise to put true heat-loving plants along southern and protected walls.

❧ Bare soil compacts quickly with all this heavy rain. When mushroom manure, a very good mulch, is mixed with leaves and sand, it will lighten up the soil most effectively. It's wisest to keep the soil mulched all the time. Without compost, clay soil becomes very hard after it dries off. Many of the garden gurus here don't believe in cultivating—it just disturbs the roots. Well-prepared soil in the first place is *de rigueur* with lots of mulch between plants. Gardening without holes seems to work wonders.

❧ It takes about five years to grow a substantial shrub. They can be moved as early as February.

❧ Bulbs can be planted in November.

❧ Overwinter plants by digging up, cutting tops back two-thirds, and placing them in a trench, and refilling with soil. The trench, 18 inches (45 centimeters) deep, should be in a protected south-facing spot and mulched if the weather is too dry. Check them in February.

❧ Any tender shrubs should, of course, be protected from eastern and northern winds that bring in cold air.

❧ Pick off the deadheads of rhododendrons but watch out for the new growth buds just below the bloom. They are making next year's flowers.

❧ Plant fruit trees in April.

Gardens hard by coastal waters also have special requirements. There is a high salt content in the air which many plants have adapted to. In spite of the warming effect of the ocean and coastal waters, wind, sand and salt can put plants under stress so choose varieties carefully.

The wind is indeed the enemy, and you

AZALEA TANCRIUM

might primarily put in plants that will act as shelters. Consider such shrubs such as ATRIPLEX, Saltbush; ACACIA LONGIFOLIA; COROKIA COTONEASTER; CYTISUS, Broom; ESCALLONIA; JUNIPERUS CHINENSIS 'Torulosis', Hollywood Juniper; LAURIS NOBILIS, Laurel; GAULTHERIA SHALLON, Salal; EUONYMUS JAPONICA, Evergreen Euonymus; ROSA RUGOSA is often called Beach Rose for good reason. POLYGONUM, Knotweed, and CEANOTHUS, California Lilac, are both attractive. TAMARIX has a fine feathery foliage that turns bright pink and succeeds best when it's cut back in spring. There are many forms of native plants that are suited to this type of garden, especially the seaside goldenrod.

SELECTED LISTINGS
FOR HARDINESS ZONE SEVEN

ACANTHUS MOLLIS (ak-AN-thus)
❧ **Bear's-breech**

An extraordinarily emphatic plant with real architectural qualities. Used by Romans and Greeks to make garlands, you can see the leaves worked into the carvings on Corinthian columns.

Uses: Make a statement with this extraordinary plant—preferably at the back of the border or as a specimen.

Maintenance: Mulch in colder zones; provide shade in hottest areas; cut stems back to ground level in early autumn, or in cold areas in early spring; propagate by root cuttings in winter or by seed in spring. Slugs like this plant—watch out for them.

Light: Full sun to partial shade.

Size: 36" - 48" (90 cm - 120 cm) high, 24" - 36" (60 cm - 90 cm) wide.

Color: Large leaves are dark green, hairy and deeply cut; flower spikes are crowded with mauve and white hooded blooms.

Blooms: August.

Soil: Well-drained soil.

Watering: Hates winter damp; keep moist in summer, but will tolerate some drought.

Origin: Europe (Mediterranean).

ARUM MACULATUM (AY-rum)
❧ **Lords-and-ladies**

Another splendid spring show. The foliage comes out in late summer, stays all winter and disappears after flowering. I love the callalike bloom.

Uses: Good for winter contrast; combine with HELLEBORUS ORIENTALIS, GALANTHUS or Snowdrops, and other early flowers and ground covers; open woodland gardens; naturalizes in grass; good cut flower.

Maintenance: Another plant that slugs will devour; propagate by division in spring or by separating offsets and replanting them.

Light: Full sun to partial shade.

Size: 18" (45 cm) high, 12" (30 cm) wide.

Color: Long petiolate leaves with pale green midribs; long, pale greenish spathes; red berries.

Blooms: April to May.

Soil: Rich moist deep soil.

Watering: Keep moist.

Origin: Southeastern Europe.

Bear's-breech *see* ACANTHUS MOLLIS

Cape Colony Nerine *see* NERINE BOWDENII

Common White Jasmine *see* JASMINUM OFFICINALE

CYCLAMEN PERSICUM (SIK-la-men) ❧

A member of the primrose family. The florist's type is familiar but they are not the hardy little species of the woodland garden.

Uses: Good for woodland or wild garden; best under protection of large shrubs or trees; combine with heathers.

Maintenance: Set corms 1 inch (2.5 centimeters) to 2 inches (5 centimeters) beneath surface of soil, 3 inches (15 centimeters) apart; shelter from hot sun and winds; leave undisturbed; propagate by seed sown when ripe or in fall. Seedlings take about two years to flower.

Light: Partial shade.

Size: 8" (20 cm) high.

Color: Ranges from pure white to pink to crimson.

Blooms: December to March.

Soil: Humus-rich, well-drained limy soil.

Watering: Moist.

Origin: Southeast Europe, Asia minor.

JASMINUM OFFICINALE (JAS-minnum) ❧ **Common White Jasmine**

The magnificent scent, ability to clamber over whatever is offered, and early blooming make this a special plant.

Uses: Excellent for porches, arbors, trellised fences; combine it with clematis.

Maintenance: Protect growing plants in winter; tie up shoots for support; prune after blooming by thinning out tangled shoots; propagate by cutting and keeping under glass in late summer, early fall.

Light: Full sun to partial shade.

Size: 30' (9 m) high.

Color: Petite white primrose-like flowers set on elegant green leaves.

Blooms: June to October.

Soil: Any fertile, well-drained soil.

Watering: Keep slightly moist.

Origin: Asia.

Lords-and-ladies *see* ARUM MACULATUM

MIMULUS (MIM-yew-lus), ❧ **Monkey Flower**

A cheerful addition to any flower border.

(Zone 8) Kathie Leishman's superb pond and garden is a metaphor for the lushness of these zones:
IRIS SIBIRICA; CORNUS STOLONIFERA; TAXUS, *Juniper;* AZALEA GHENT, *Japanese Maple; Juniper;* IRIS
PSEUDACORUS, *yellow Iris with* ACONITUM *'Ivorine';* PINACEAE.

Uses: Colonize in damp areas beside water; a wonderful ground cover; combine with heather for a late spring show.

Maintenance: Remove stems as blooms fade to encourage further blooming and to prevent self-seeding; can run rampant in damp areas; propagate by division.

Light: Full sun to partial shade.

Size: 12" (30 cm) high, 12" (30 cm) wide.

Color: From scarlet to vivid yellow blooms above low mats of foliage.

Blooms: May to August.

Soil: Permanently moist soil.

Watering: Keep moist.

Origin: Chile.

Monkey Flower see MIMULUS

NERINE BOWDENII (ne-RY-ne)
🌱 **Cape Colony Nerine**
Freshens up the late summer and fall garden when everything else is looking a bit sad.

Uses: A potted plant except in the mildest location; excellent balcony plant.

Maintenance: After blooming the foliage goes brown; bring inside to a bright window or greenhouse. When it dies back let the bulbs rest until early fall; propagate by offsets or division in spring.

Light: Full sun.

Size: 24" (60 cm) high.

Color: Long bare stems with six blooms of pink in various tones rise above straplike stems.

Blooms: September to November.

Soil: Any well-drained soil will do.

Watering: Keep moist.

Origin: South Africa.

SELECTED LISTINGS FOR
HARDINESS ZONES EIGHT AND NINE

AGAPANTHUS AFRICANUS
(ag-a-PAN-thus) ❧ **Lily-of-the-Nile**
Tuberous herbs that provide a gorgeous display for the late summer garden. They attract butterflies.

Uses: Good tub growers on patios or porches or in small gardens; it makes a striking specimen in the garden; well paired with ACHILLEA FILIPENDULINA or with LYCHNIS CORONARIA.

Maintenance: If grown in tubs it will need constant fertilizing after a few seasons—they are gross feeders; set crowns 2 inches (5 centimeters) deep, 15 inches (40 centimeters) apart; in cold areas cover with good mulch; cut back to ground level in fall; do not disturb roots; propagate by division in spring.

Light: Full sun.

(Zone 9) Susan Ryley's lovely border by the pool.
Left to right above the wall: PYRUS SALICIFOLIA PENDULA, *Willow Leaf Pear Tree; in the pots are variegated boxwood; and in the courtyard,* GERANIUM SANGUINEUM, *var.* LANCASTRENSE.

Size: 24" (60 cm) high.

Color: Masses of sword-shaped leaves with tall spikes of funnel-shaped blue flowers smother each stalk—up to 30 on each.

Blooms: July to September.

Soil: Good, well-drained soil; will tolerate lime.

Watering: Keep moist.

Origin: Africa.

California Fuschia *see* ZAUSCHNERIA CALIFORNICA

Calla Lily *see* ZANTEDESCHIA AETHIOPICA

HEBE PINGUIFOLIA (HEE-bee) ❧ **Veronica**

A shrubby veronica (another great big family), evergreen and good looking.

Uses: Ground cover; good for coastal areas since it tolerates salt spray; plant in pots in colder regions.

Maintenance: Shelter in more extreme areas away from the coast; plant 15 inches (40 centimeters) to 18 inches (45 centimeters) apart for ground cover; propagate by late summer cuttings or remove any rooted shoots and replant; do not prune. Do not despair if it disappears in a sharp winter. It may come back from the roots.

Light: Full sun to partial shade.

Size: 6" (15 cm) high, 24" (60 cm) wide.

Color: Carpet of grey-blue leaves with spikes of small white flowers.

Blooms: May to June.

Soil: Well-drained soil.

Watering: Keep very moist.

Origin: New Zealand.

Lily of the Nile *see* AGAPANTHUS AFRICANUS

Veronica *see* HEBE PINGUIFOLIA

ZANTEDESCHIA AETHIOPICA (zan-tee-DESH-ia) ❧ **Calla Lily**

This gorgeous plant has now become a familiar sight in mild areas near water. It is the most elegant of all plants.

Uses: Always looks great beside water—pond, lake or river where the roots can be kept free from frost. Perfect in the shady garden.

Maintenance: Protect crowns with mulch in winter or lift and store in pots, or in a greenhouse until spring; propagate by division in spring.

Light: Full sun to partial shade.

Size: 36" - 48" (90 cm -120 cm) high, 12" - 24" (30 cm - 60 cm) wide.

Color: Large creamy white blooms over glossy arrow-shaped deep green leaves.

Blooms: June to August.

Soil: Well-drained, especially in winter; good soil but not over-rich.

Watering: Keep consistently moist.

Origin: South Africa.

ZAUSCHNERIA CALIFORNICA (Zaush-NEAR-ia) ❧ **California Fuschia**

A splendid late-blooming plant for the informal garden.

Uses: Good if space is unlimited; on a wall, near a bank or any very dry place. This one is drought resistant; good specimen plant.

Maintenance: Not for cold or exposed gardens; mulch in winter —cover crowns; propagate in early summer by basal cuttings, root and overwinter under glass.

Light: Full sun.

Size: 12" - 36" (30 cm - 90 cm) high, 18" (45 cm) wide.

Color: Scarlet and magenta flowers with green, green foliage. It might overwinter as an evergreen in very mild areas.

Blooms: September to October.

Soil: Well-drained.

Watering: Tolerates some drought.

Origin: California.

More plants for Zones 7, 8, 9

ALSTROEMERIA AURANTIACA, **Yellow Alstroemeria**
AMARYLLIS BELLADONNA, **Belladonna-lily**
AMSONIA CILIATA, **Blue-star**
GLADIOLUS BYZANTUS, **Sword Lily**
GUNNERA MANICATA
PASSIFLORA CAERULEA, **Common Passion Flower**
PHYGELIUS CAPENSIS, **Cape-fuschia**
SOLANUM CRISPUM, **Chilean Potato Tree**
STERNBERGIA LUTEA, **Fall-daffodil**

GLOSSARY

Acid soil: Soil with a pH content below 7.0; the more acid the soil, the lower it is on a scale measured from 1 to 9. Areas with heavy rainfall will probably be more acidic than those with little rain.

Aerial roots: Roots on such climbers as HYDRANGEA PETIOLARIS which are self-clinging; roots formed above ground.

Alkaline soil: Soil that measures from 7.1 to 9 has a sweeter or more limy content, usually found in arid places.

Alpine plant: A rock garden plant usually found in mountainous regions above the tree line.

Annual: A plant which grows roots, stems, flowers and sets seeds in one year and doesn't return unless it self-seeds.

Axil: The angle between a stem and a leaf growing from it.

Basal cutting: Cutting taken from the base of the plant.

Bed: An area for flowers usually in the middle of a garden.

Bedding plants: Usually refers to annuals used in beds or borders.

Biennial: Herbaceous plant that puts up foliage in the first year, blooms and dies in the second year. Some may self-seed which gives the sense that they are perennial.

Border: An area for plants usually, but not necessarily, at the side of a garden.

Bract: A leaf at the base of a flower which protects the forming flower.

Bud: The beginning of a flower protected by overlapping scales.

Bulb, bulbil: A modified bud with swollen base which stores food for the following year. Bulbil is a smaller version. Tulips come from bulbs.

Callus: Tissue formed when a twig, stem or leaf is cut.

Canopy: The tops of trees that provide shade.

Chelated iron: Used to treat plants stricken with chlorosis (turning yellow).

Cloche: Cone of plastic that acts as a mini-greenhouse for tender plants.

Chlorosis: When a plant cannot manufacture enough green color and turns yellow.

Compost: Decomposed organic matter.

Corm: A food storage unit found underground at the base of the stem. A crocus comes from a corm.

Cotyledon: Seed leaf.

Crown: The upper part of a stem. Shoots grow from it.

Cultivar: Variety of species developed by cultivation.

Cultivator: Tool with tines to scratch the earth.

Cutting: The part of a plant taken from the parent to make a new plant—from stems, roots or leaves—cut cleanly from the mother plant and placed in a rooting medium (sand, sphagnum moss, vermiculite or a combination).

Damping-Off: Molds causing injury to seedlings.

Deadheading: Removing faded or dying blossoms to prevent a flower from forming seeds; method of encouraging perennials and annuals to flower again.

Deciduous: Plants whose leaves die off—usually in the fall.

Dormancy: Resting state of a plant.

Drift: Plants of same species planted in large groups.

Earthing up: Piling earth around a plant to protect it in winter.

Espalier: Method of training plants along fences or wires by selecting out lateral branches and removing all others.

Evergreen: Plant that keeps its foliage all year round.

Eye: Undeveloped bud on a tuber; bloom with a different color center.

Family: A group of plants sharing basic characteristics.

Fertilizer: Material needed to assist in plant health. Can be chemical but organic are far better; may be blood and bone meal (singly or combined), phosphate or superphosphate, or compost.

Foliage plant: Plants grown mainly for their leaves rather than for flowers.

Friable: Crumbly soil.

Gazebo: A small open house set apart in the garden.

Genus: One or many closely related species; plural is genera.

Germination: The development of a small plant from seed under optimum conditions.

Glaucous: Grey-green or blue foliage.

Green manure: A specially-planted fast growing crop used to improve the quality of poor soil.

Ground cover: Plants that spread laterally across the ground.

Habitat: A place or part of the country where a plant originates, such as a swamp or desert.

Hardening off: The process of acclimatizing a plant to colder temperatures outside a house or greenhouse.

Hardiness: The quality of a plant to withstand low temperatures, and other climatic considerations, such as elevation or wind velocity. Half-hardy plants need winter protection.

Heel-cutting: Offshoot taken from the main branch: the heel is a small piece on the outside of the old stem 1/2 inch (1.25 centimeter) long. When it's trimmed, callus tissue forms and it will root in ordinary soil.

Heeling in: Covering a plant's roots with soil in a temporary place such as a trench.

Herbaceous: A perennial that dies down in winter to soil level, comes back in spring.

Herbicide: A chemical which kills herbaceous plants such as weeds.

Humus: Decaying organic matter such as leaf mold.

Hybrid: The offspring of two plants that have been crossbred.

Inflorescence: Flower clusters.

Internode: Length between leaves or buds.

Interplant: The custom of planting small plants among larger ones.

Island bed: A bed away from the edges of a garden.

Knot garden: A very old form of gardening in which one small edging plant such as BUXUS is planted so that it forms an intricate design, traditionally in a love-knot form.

Lateral: The part of a plant that grows away from the main stem of a plant from a bud.

Layering: Rooting of a lower branch of a plant while still attached to the parent plant.

Leaching: Any medium that flows through soil taking nutrients away.

Leader: The major or first shoot on a

shrub or tree.

Leaf mold: Fallen leaves in the process of decaying.

Lime: Calcium carbonate, which most plants need to grow properly; added to heavy soil it improves the texture and reduces the amount of acidity in the soil.

Loggia: A open air arcade—Italian originally—a shady walk.

Microclimate: Local climate near the ground; most gardens have several microclimates in them depending on the prevailing wind, elevation and density of shade.

Monocarpic: A plant that dies after it blooms. AGAVES may take up to 50 years before they bloom and then die.

Mulch: A medium spread around plants, but not touching the stem, that cuts down the development of weeds, keeps soil moist and healthy by breaking down slowly, and enriches the soil in the process.

Naturalize: A plant which will reproduce itself and spread.

Nematode: Microscopic worms that usually feed on roots; some, however, feed on leaves. If a plant is infected with nematodes, it's best to destroy it.

Neutral soil: Soil with a pH content of 7.0.

Nitrogen (N): an element crucial to the development and health of a plant. Not enough nitrogen means the plant gets yellow and scraggly; too much and it develops weak stems and flops.

Node: The point along the stem where a branch or leaf forms.

Nodule: Pealike growths on the roots of legumes.

Offset: Small plantlets or bulblets growing off the parent plant or bulb.

Organic matter: Anything that's alive with bacterial content.

Parterre: A traditional area of a garden resembling an outside room; an area surrounded by hedges so that it extends the feeling of the house. French in origin where the design was meant to be viewed from above.

Peat moss: Partially decomposed mosses; sphagnum peat moss is more acidic than other peats. This is a water-retention medium with little food value. Never apply dry peat—soak it up to a week starting with hot water.

Peat Garden: A acidic damp garden made of peaty soil ideal for woodland plants.

Perennial: Plant that lives for two or more years which is either woody or herbaceous.

Pergola: A wooden structure of pillars and crossbeams usually with vines growing over it.

Petiole: Leaf stalk.

pH: Potential hydrogen or concentration of hydrogen ions in the soil. It is usually followed by a number, pH 7 for instance, to indicate the acidity or alkalinity of the soil. A pH level of 7 indicates neutral soil.

Phosphate (P): A chemical necessary for plant health. Without it a plant tends to develop in a spindly manner.

Pistil: Seed-producing organ of the flower.

Pleaching: A method of weaving branches together to form an arbor in a formal garden. Pleached lime trees were common at one time.

Pollarding: Cutting back limbs of a tree in a drastic way to form large knubbly ends. This is done with plane trees.

Prick out: Transfer seedlings from a germination medium into pots or beds where they'll grow.

Propagation: Increasing plants by a number of methods including seeds or vegetatively—layering, cuttings, grafting, rhizomes—which produce exact replicas of the parent plant. Seeds do not necessarily reproduce exactly the same each time.

Pruning: Take out stems and branches or roots to get rid of dead parts or to reshape a plant.

Ramping: A short form gardeners like to use meaning to run rampant or spread wildly.

Rhizome: Underground horizontal stem.

Root crown: The base of the stem or top of a thick taproot crowned with leaves.

Rosette: Basal cluster of leaves attached to the root crown.

Runner: A thin stem sent out by some perennials—sometimes refers to a stolon—at the end of which an offshoot develops.

Scarification: Abrading the surface of seed to make it germinate by nicking, cutting or filing.

Scree: Small rock from rock outcroppings. In the garden it's used for growing alpines.

Secateurs: Pruning shears.

Sepal: Leaflike green appendages outside the petals of a flower.

Sessile: Without a stalk.

Softwood: Twigs of current year's growth.

Species: One consistent kind of plant from generation to generation. It is the second word in a plant's name.

Specimen: A plant that is used on its own for ornamental value rather than as part of a border; or a tree or a shrub used on its own.

Sport: A shoot from a single bud that differs from the parent.

Standard: Any plant grown into a small treelike form with a single trunk with round top of flowers or leaves. Many standards are top-grafted.

Stem cutting: Cutting taken from the stem of the parent plant and rooted to form a new plant.

Stolon: Runner between plants at ground level that develops roots at intervals.

Stratification: Treatment with heat or cold to break a seed's dormancy.

Subshrub: Small shrub usually under 3 feet (1 meter) high.

Succulent: Fleshy-textured plants that tend to like arid conditions.

Sucker: Growth from the original root of a shrub.

Superphosphate: An inorganic fertilizer providing necessary phosphors.

Taproot: The main root that grows straight down, usually deeper than all the other root systems.

Tender: A plant with low tolerance to cold.

Tilth: The crumbly quality of the soil.

Topdress: Applying manure or compost to the surface around a plant without digging it in.

Topiary: Cutting trees and shrubs into ornamental shapes.

Variety: The variant of a species that is given a name—cultivars.

Vegetative cuttings: Cutting from roots or shoots of a parent plant for propagation that doesn't involve fertilization from seed.

Vista: A long narrow view usually toward a specific plant or object in the garden.

Woody: Evergreen or deciduous trees, shrubs or vines that stay alive during the dormant season.

BIBLIOGRAPHY

Aden, Paul, ed. *The Hosta Book.* Portland, Or.: Timber, 1988

Ball, Jeff. *Rodale's Garden Problem Solver.* Emmaus, Pa.: Rodale Press, 1988

Barr, Claude A. *Jewels of the Plains.* Minneapolis: University of Minnesota Press, 1983

Biles, Roy Edwin. *The Complete Book of Garden Magic.* Chicago: J. G. Ferguson, 1953

Birdseye, Clarence and Eleanor Birdseye. *Growing Woodland Plants.* New York: Dover, [1972]

Briggs, Chriss D. *Plant Magic for Northern Gardens.* Northern News Services Ltd. and Dept. of Information, Government of Northwest Territories, 1979

Brookes, John. *The Country Garden Book.* New York: Crown, 1987

—. *The Small Garden.* New York: Crown, 1989

Charlesworth, Geoffrey. *The Opinionated Gardener.* Boston: Godine, 1987

Chatto, Beth. *The Dry Garden.* London: J. M. Dent, 1983

Clausen, Ruth Rogers and Nicholas H. Ekstrom. *Perennials For American Gardens.* New York: Random, 1989.

Cox, Jeff and Marilyn Cox. *The Perennial Garden.* Emmaus, Pa.: Rodale Press, 1985

Druse, Ken. *The Natural Garden.* New York: Clarkson N. Potter Books, 1989

Fish, Margery. *Gardening in the Shade.* London; Boston: Faber and Faber, 1984

Fox, Robin Lane. *Variations on a Garden.* Boston: Godine, 1987

—. *Better Gardening.* Boston: Godine, 1986

Garland, Sarah. *The Herb Garden.* Harmondsworth: Penguin, 1985

Hill, Lewis. *Cold Climate Gardening.* Pownal, Vermont: Garden Way Publishing, 1987

Hobhouse, Penelope. *Colour in Your Garden.* Boston: Little, Brown, 1985

—. *Garden Style.* Little, Brown, 1988

Illustrated Guide to Gardening in Canada. Montreal: Reader's Digest, 1978

Jekyll, Gertrude. *Making of a Garden.* Woodbridge, Suffolk: Antique Collectors' Club, 1984

—. *Wall Water Gardens.* Salem, N.H.: The Ayer Company, 1984

—. *Colour Schemes for the Flower Garden.* Woodbridge, Suffolk: Antique Collectors' Club, 1984

Johnson, Hugh. *The Principles of Gardening.* London: M. Beazley, 1984

Keeble, Midge Ellis. *Tottering in My Garden.* Camden East: Camden House, 1989

Kruckeberg, Arthur. *Gardening with Native Plants of the Pacific Northwest.* Vancouver: Douglas & McIntyre, 1982

Lacy, Stephen. *The Startling Jungle.* New York: Viking, 1986

Lima, Patrick. *The Harrowsmith Perennial Garden.* Camden East: Camden House, 1987

Lloyd, Christopher. *The Adventurous Gardener.* New York: Random House, 1985

—. *Foliage Plants.* New York: Viking, 1988

—. *The Well-Tempered Garden.* Harmondsworth: Penguin, 1988

Ortho's Complete Guide to Successful Gardening. San Francisco: Ortho Press, 1983

Ottesen, Carole. *The New American Garden.* New York: Macmillan, 1988

Page, Russell. *The Education of a Gardener.* New York: Random House, 1985

Paterson, Allen. *Plants for Shade and Woodland.* Markham: Fitzhenry & Whiteside, 1987

Reader's Digest Guide to Creative Gardening. Montreal: Reader's Digest, 1986

Rice, Graham. *Plants for Problem Places.* Potland, Or.: Timber Press, 1988

Rodale, Robert, ed. *The Basic Book of Organic Gardening.* Emmaus, Pa.: Rodale Press, 1987

Sunset Editors. *Western Garden Magazine.* Menlo Park, Ca.: Lane, 1988

Tarrant, David. *A Year in Your Garden.* Vancouver: Whitecap Books, 1989

Vick, Rodger. *Gardening on the Prairies.* Saskatoon: Western Producer, 1987

Wilder, Louise Beebe. *The Fragrant Garden.* New York: Dover, 1974 (reprint 1936 ed.)

Willison, Marjorie, *Successful Landscape Design.* Halifax: Nimbus, 1989

REFERENCE BOOKS

Hortus Third. New York: Macmillan, 1976

Taylor's Encyclopedia of Gardening. Boston: Houghton Mifflin, 1987

Wyman, Donald. *The Gardening Encyclopedia.* New York: Macmillan, 1986

PERIODICALS

Garden Design
Gardenesque
Gardens West
Horticulture

Journal of the Ontario Rock Garden Society
Organic Gardening
The Climate for Agriculture in Atlantic Canada
The Island Grower

Trellis (Civic Garden Centre, Toronto)
Wildflower

INDEX

Page numbers in boldface denote illustrations.
Page numbers in italics are detailed descriptions.